THE INVISIBLE DOOR
Mireya Mudd

ACKNOWLEDGMENT

To my dear and loving husband Lee who has been a strong support throughout our marriage. He helped me during my severe treatments for cancer and was my compass in those troubled times. We grow closer and more in love each day.

To my Sons who inspired me with their courage to survive and become the strong people we are today.

To Nancy and Darrell who helped me edit my book and gave me insights to improve my story.

THE INVISIBLE DOOR
Mireya Mudd

INTRODUCTION

Women deserve their rightful place and space in society. In certain cultures where men rule above all others, the development of women has been held back. In such places, these aggressive and individualized men have created an environment where women are incapable of developing.

Society in many parts of the world has changed over recent years with certain cultures but there are still many cases in which women are very controlled and dominated by men.

This book will take the reader down a painful road, literally and figuratively, and you will discover how one woman fought for her individuality and her space on a day-

THE INVISIBLE DOOR
Mireya Mudd

by-day basis. In order to have saved herself, she had many adversaries to overcome, such as physical and mental abuse by her husband, the lack of economical protection and separation from her children.

When she was able to accomplish activities on an individual basis she started to value herself which opened several doors that before, she could never have imagined. She was able to be valued, became self sufficient and was appreciated by everyone.

To this one determined woman, there was an *invisible door* which stopped her from seeing the other side, and when she crossed through that door she overcame barriers that before were unreachable. Opening that invisible door created the path to her freedom and where she found her true self.

Here is her story.

THE INVISIBLE DOOR
Mireya Mudd

CHAPTER ONE
July 18, 1999

Since that day Ana Laura stopped seeing him with the same loving eyes, everything was lost.

Her ears could not understand the inconsistency of what she was hearing from him. Her physical body and mind were in a state of agitation and she did not want to understand these differing sensations. It had been eight years of marriage with Paul, her second husband, and everything was falling apart.

Ana Laura had always wanted to have a tranquil marriage, full of happiness and promises. She believed she deserved it. Her hopes and dreams on how life should be were never confusing to her, but now she was realizing that

THE INVISIBLE DOOR
Mireya Mudd

everything was more complicated than what she thought. Everything she understood about life was unrealistic. She had followed a false belief and in reality she had not experienced anything in life. In other words, she thought that bad things only could happen to people with bad intentions. Thinking with that belief while she grew up, she had always felt safe. Her ignorance and immaturity had taken her to a point where she perceived everything around her in an idealistic way. Now she knew she had not experienced anything in life. Now she knew she was an unrealistic thinker. After a few years into her second marriage she started to understand that she lived in a fantasy and that real life was very different.

With time she saw things with a different perspective. Since confronting life and suffering in an unbearable way she could see things more objectively.

Now nobody or anything could protect her from her marriage with Paul, neither her social class, nor her family prestige, nor her false hopes of idealizing love in an absurd way. Reality of daily living was opening the evidence of

THE INVISIBLE DOOR
Mireya Mudd

what was happening to her.

On that one night she tried to avoid her first nightmare. Was it a dream? Was that dream real? What she had passed through, what she had heard, with actions that hurt her badly. Those words were said with the intention of hurting and those words had helped her see her situation in a more realistic way. That night she felt Paul's body beside her, but for the first time an unbreakable barrier interrupted their contact.

When she became conscious, a hammering in her head was repeating those words: "I won't allow this to ever happen again."

"What do you mean?" Paul asked. Ana Laura answered that she could not understand what he was saying.

Paul continued. "My stepmother abused my father economically. She robbed him of his money and now she wants to rob us the little bit that he left us. She is taking the case to court in order to keep the house, the one, she knows, was bought between the two of them, and she is not the complete owner. But of course," he continued, "because my father left a bad estate testament, now, we have to fight for our inheritance."

"Of course, my father trusted her good faith, but let me tell you this; this won't ever happen again. Tomorrow I am changing my papers so that all my retirement money goes to my children." replied Paul.

Those words were like a bucket full of cold water that Ana Laura felt dropping on her shoulders, and this was the man that she was married to for eight years, the man that she shared her bed with for so long?

Paul, who had helped get her out of a very bad and abusive situation with her first husband, Ramiro, was now treating her like his worst enemy. She tried to excuse him, since her love for him was immense and she told herself that she was sure Paul was only projecting her stepmother's life on herself. Paul was that man who had motivated her to continue studying in order to become independent; was that man who Ana Laura admired as nobody else and for whom she would have given her life, the one Ana Laura glorified and venerated blindly, now talked of a big distrust of her.

THE INVISIBLE DOOR
Mireya Mudd

That distrust was something that she could not explain. Ana Laura tried to excuse his thinking, telling herself that Paul must be passing through a severe crisis since his father just passed away. She tried to understand him.

She forced herself to be reasonable but a deep anger was building all over her body and her thoughts began to overpower her reasonableness. Ana Laura talked to herself. *Who does he think he is to treat me like that? I don't need the little money that he can inherit to me. After all, I don't really care about the money but who will give me back that immense love I gave to Paul?* Yes, Ana Laura loved him and idolized him and did not have the least idea of wanting to lose him.

Since a long time ago, she felt that he was uncomfortable and not very happy living with her. One time, she asked Paul. "Tell me, why do you always arrive home quietly and play solitary and don't want to talk? Is there something I have done to you?" When she asked, she got a deep silence from him, followed with only her own personal hurt.

THE INVISIBLE DOOR
Mireya Mudd

Sometimes she noticed him playing cards for hours and hours and that was worrying her since communication was cut. She remembers Paul's answer was, "Married life is less nourishing and less bearable than single life. One does everything with one person and everything becomes monotonous and a routine (more or less). Most people live with another person not for the company, but for fear of living alone." Paul continued "…and this makes the couple less spiritually rich. They get stuck and don't grow anymore inside. Any problems confronted and they believe they won't be able to solve it themselves, that they require help from the other person, and as I said before, they don't grow spiritually and create a codependency." This comment was confirmed by Paul with his writing philosophy.

Now Ana Laura began to understand everything. Paul was a person to be by himself, not to be married. Before meeting her, he had been divorced for sixteen years, while she was living with her first husband, Ramiro, the same amount of years and with her children Rodrigo and Andrés.

THE INVISIBLE DOOR
Mireya Mudd

Anyhow, Ana Laura had lived very happy in her second marriage until she noticed Paul's attitude changing and this started to affect everything.

During her married life with Paul, Ana Laura had much enjoyment with plenty of freedom. She understood that this enjoyment factor did not guarantee her happiness because it took two people for the relationship to work.

There was no human power she possessed that could change Paul's attitude and this was very painful for her. If she only could start again and be less possessive but it was not that easy and now it was too late. By this time there was no doubt in her mind how difficult it was to conduct a relationship.

THE INVISIBLE DOOR
Mireya Mudd

CHAPTER TWO
A day of terror

One cloudy evening, Ana Laura was sitting at the riverside in Petersburg, West Virginia, where Paul's and her little house was located. Ana Laura was alone with her thoughts and she began to remember how somehow not in a far past that she had left an elevated social position. She had resigned all her belongings and inheritance to obtain her freedom and subsequently obtained a legal settlement with her first husband, Ramiro. He was an extreme controller, had been very jealous, who mistreated and abused her physically for sixteen years, and at the same time had managed to keep their children away from her.

* * *

Ana Laura could not forget how humiliated she felt during her first marriage on repeated occasions and could not avoid remembering the terrible days she was still married to Ramiro.

THE INVISIBLE DOOR
Mireya Mudd

Her baby Andrés was only one year old and they lived in Oregon, USA, where Ramiro was studying to become a musician.

Ana Laura remembered how she felt so isolated because her activities were limited to a small apartment.

On days when Ramiro left for school, Ana Laura asked to leave her the car to go somewhere with the baby. Instead, he would order her to remain at home saying. "I already told you that the car is there so that I can use it to study. I don't want the baby to catch a cold so I want you to remain here and don't go out under any excuse to the open air."

Unfortunately the weather didn't help with her situation. It snowed often and was extremely cold, so she couldn't take Andrés out anywhere. Her life with Ramiro continued being a nightmare full of authoritarian and absurd rules where her word didn't count at all and her development as a person had been blocked absurdly. Ana Laura felt like her personality was taken away and she knew she had so much to give.

THE INVISIBLE DOOR
Mireya Mudd

Ana Laura could see many mothers taking their babies out, well covered, and, on the contrary, she needed to stay enclosed in a little apartment without communication from anyone, not even with her family, since they lived in Mexico and she was five thousand miles away from them.

Every Sunday Ana Laura got a phone call from her parents, and she felt incapable of telling them the truth, since she knew that the distance in miles blocked any kind of communication. If she would have told them her situation, she would have made them feel incapable, frustrated and would have involved them in her suffering without them being capable of helping her. So, instead, she remained quiet in her own pain.

The only transportation was a little Oldsmobile and Ramiro took it with him everyday to the university, leaving her alone with the baby. His selfishness was unlimited and Ana Laura knew in reality that he wanted to control her in all her actions. She was in a foreign country where she had no friends or family or any social network, where she could not study at school and did not work a paying job. She was alone with her baby in an intimidating world and hours passed very slowly until Ramiro came back from the university. When he returned her situation was even worse since she needed to deal with his bad temper and his abuses. Her life was set to be alone with her baby and to be unloved by her spouse. Her life was a controlled routine full of obligations but no appreciation or love.

Ana Laura felt like she was suffocating with little air and what was given, she could not breathe. Her freedom was being trounced upon and she was determined to talk to Ramiro. She remembered how she never wanted to be a victim and how she had defended her rights as a woman up until her marriage. She wanted to work and study. She knew her capacity for development was immense and that she was not just an object of decoration.

Every time she had the opportunity to mention this to her husband, the conversation became a battle where Ana Laura clearly knew it was worthless to complain, neither to negotiate nor to gather an agreement. Her wishes were always blocked by the authoritarian and irrational wish of her husband. It did not take long to realize that her voice was mute and her will nor her person counted for anything. Neither her wishes nor aspirations mattered for in a few words her husband took all the decisions concerning the household or their son without asking for advice from her.

It took her a few months to realize it was better to avoid conflicts and conform, but difficult not to contradict him since her rights were ignored and humiliated.

When Ramiro came back from the university, she always had dinner ready and usually he was coming back in a very bad mood, like many occasions, so, nothing new.

Seeing this day after day of bad moods and the unloving situation in which he treated her, his lack of love and affection and his authoritarian temper, her loneliness grew day by day. She daydreamed about having a normal marriage, full of love and understanding, where she could be kissed and where he would have told her how much he missed her.

Most evenings, her thoughts were interrupted when he asked, "What's for dinner?" She thought about

THE INVISIBLE DOOR
Mireya Mudd

contradicting him to see if they could go out for a while, since the morning had been long and she needed some fresh air. Maybe he would take her to the drive in movie since that was the only place he wanted to go so that the baby didn't get cold.

So, she answered. "Lentils soup, pork stew with rice and vegetables."

"Well, in that case, serve me, but quickly since I am very hungry." She served him quickly knowing when he was hungry it was best not to argue. She never liked his authoritarian tone and tried to avoid thinking about a better life even though her feelings of lost love were impossible to avoid. Now she saw him as a jailer who tortured and contradicted her and it was very difficult for her to show affection for that man who was her husband. Her dreams and wishes could not be contained anymore.

On the occasion in question, when he tasted the soup he shouted. "What is this?" Spitting the soup he continued screaming! "The soup is boiling mother f….. You know better. I don't like it so hot and I know you did it on purpose," Before she could respond she felt the hot soup on her face and body.

"How about this?" as he spilled all the soup on her. "F......bitch, see if you like it this hot... Hee...Hee! You do all this because you know I don't like it like this, right?" Pointing with his finger at Ana Laura, he threatens her, "You got me up to my limit and I am not going to tolerate this anymore." She could see the brightened anger in his eyes and knew he could not control himself, just like so many other occasions.

Ana Laura feels the boiling soup on her body and face and now she boils over in anger saying. "Look, you are the one that has tied me up. You keep me here enclosed without letting me go anywhere, enclosed without being able to study or do anything and now this…!"

"Listen," he interrupted, "you bitch, you chose to have a baby and now you go fuck yourself," and saying this he turned around and ignored her.

She starts to cry inconsolably and gets into the shower with clothes on to wash off the mess. While she is rinsing

THE INVISIBLE DOOR
Mireya Mudd

all the soup from her clothes she feels Ramiro nearby. Jumping nervously from him he pulls her out of the shower and slaps her on her face, then throws her toward the wall making a hole in it and shouts.

"Mother f.......you got me up to my limit, either you straighten yourself up, or you will need to deal with me."

Ramiro doesn't stop slapping Ana Laura. Then the baby started crying. She can hear him crying in his cradle and she is incapable of defending herself. If I was stronger....she thinks.

Ramiro isn't over the humiliation and hurt and wants to continue with the fight.

This out of control man treats Ana Laura sadistically as if he cannot stop. She is terrified. "And now you are going to hear me," he continued, "Let's see if this teaches you how to behave with me. Do you want to continue the battle? Eh? eh? Is this what you want? Well let's see what we can get out of this......eh?" Pointing with his finger like it was a weapon. "How do you see this daughter of your f....... mother?"

THE INVISIBLE DOOR
Mireya Mudd

Ana Laura cannot believe he has inflicted so much cruelty. One thing she knows is that this person who dares calls himself a husband and father is not going to abuse her anymore. Pretty soon she feels stronger, stronger than ever. She knows she has to do something to avoid these abuses that have been happening since she got married.

Ramiro leaves angry, but not without slamming the door. The baby continued crying without stopping for even the baby sensed the aggressions and the chaos. Ana Laura ran towards the baby crying too. Reaching the cradle she holds the baby to console him and both cry together to release the tension. While she is holding him she starts thinking. She feels inside a gated cell, humiliated, incapable of doing anything, without money and no protection. What could she do in a foreign country and away from the people who loved her? Who can help her? She cried all night long thinking what she should do. Which solution can this situation have so she doesn't get stepped over again?

THE INVISIBLE DOOR
Mireya Mudd

She hears the door slamming. He's back and she feels terror and doesn't know how to react. The best is to pretend that she is sleeping. She hears him smoking in the living room and walking from one side to the other. That room has become his personal dormitory, since many months ago he had decided to not sleep in the bedroom, since *the icicle* or the brat (the way he called the baby) wakes him up. The woman hears him smoking, perceives the smell of the smoke which goes all the way to the bedroom. She notices the television stays on until two in the morning. Ana Laura doesn't want to see him at all anymore. She feels repulsion while smelling his cigarette and now all the love she used to feel for him has transformed into hate. When she listens to his steps in the other room she feels intimidated. She has left the sweater full of soup intentionally in the laundry basket which is in the living room. She has done this on purpose so that when Ramiro sees it, he can see it and repent on how bad he has treated her.

Even though she doesn't care anymore, after crying all night and analyzing how she has wasted her life, she has a

THE INVISIBLE DOOR
Mireya Mudd

plan, a plan toward their liberation, for she and her child to go away from this prison and start a new life.

That invisible door looks more attractive than ever, yes, that door towards her liberation is a big temptation. It becomes very attractive because now it is not so invisible anymore. She feels empowered; her liberation with her baby is close.

Next day her husband leaves the apartment angry again, not without forgetting to slam the door. Ana Laura knows this is the opportunity she was waiting for and now is the time. She needs to leave immediately with her baby Andrés.

CHAPTER THREE
Decision time

After that night, full of tears, when Ana Laura remembers so many insults and aggressions, she knows that to be with that man is now impossible.

On that night, feeling herself full of strength, she has taken the determination of going back home to Mexico with her baby.

On that Tuesday, when Ramiro left for the university, she comes out carrying her baby. She leaves the apartment urgently and goes to her neighbors asking for help. They try to persuade her in staying.

The neighbors talk to her saying, "But, Ana Laura, are you sure about this? Have you already thought about the consequences? Is that what you want for you and your baby? We don't understand. What did he do to you? We know we see you very little, but tell us, what happened?"

She is mute, she knows there are no words to describe her life full of abuses and mistreatments and at this point she doesn't have the energy or the will to explain her life with Ramiro. She just wants out as soon as possible. She knows time is precious and she doesn't want the man to come back and find out she is leaving.

So, she answers. "In reality I don't want to explain. It will take hours and I just cannot talk about this for a long time. I hope you don't take it wrong but this subject is very delicate for me, and I just don't want to explain all of this. I just want to go far away and forget everything. Also, I need to act quickly because I am afraid he will come back soon. I need to go away with my son and forget everything. I will damn the day I met Ramiro and married him. How could I have done this to myself? How could I have been so blind?" While Ana Laura was telling this to her neighbors, she was in a state full of tension and anxiety and she was incapable of talking reasonably.

She knows it is very hard for them to understand her life. She has kept it a secret, pretending every time something happened with her husband and now it was very late, nobody would understand. The only one that understands what has happened is herself.

THE INVISIBLE DOOR
Mireya Mudd

"But, his mood could be something temporary, don't you think, Ana Laura?" his neighbor insists. "Maybe this makes him react and he might change. Maybe you could consult a marriage counselor and fix your differences."

No suggestions can convince her and she cannot remain in that house. She is the only one who knows the situation and nobody else. The situation now is intolerable.

The *Invisible Door* was becoming little by little more attractive.

That evening, at two o'clock, she departs from her neighbor's home and runs home to pack. They promise to take her to Moorefield where a plane is available to take her and her child home to Mexico.

Ana Laura knows Ramiro is coming at three in the afternoon, so she hurries; in less than an hour she packs everything she can in a suitcase, runs to another neighbor to give her the borrowed baby cradle. In less than an hour the other neighbor picks her and Andres up and drives them to Moorefield.

Ana Laura has to accelerate everything. She doesn't want to be caught by Ramiro, cannot waste any time. She is scared of being caught, so she begs her neighbor to keep her secret and don't tell him of her location so she can reach her objective.

Immediately after arriving, once Ana Laura is in the hotel, she decides to call her father. She explains how Ramiro has mistreated her and how she has been abused for all these months and years like if she was Ramiro's worst enemy.

Her father cannot perceive the situation once he hears his daughter's words. She hears confusion in her father's replies.

"Dad, I wanted to tell you I am coming back with Andrés to Mexico."

"Of course daughter, we would love to see you. You know you are always welcome here," and then he continues. "For how long are you planning to visit us?"

Ana Laura knows her father doesn't understand. She has not complained all these years because she knows it

THE INVISIBLE DOOR
Mireya Mudd

wouldn't do any good. In a long distance it is hard to communicate problems. Also she knows she stayed with Ramiro just for the baby, but this abuse was crossing her limit.

"No, Dad," she continues, "you don't understand, my coming back is permanent, and I cannot tolerate to be mistreated by Ramiro anymore. Now he has stroked me and beat me and pushed me around, I am tired. This is no life."

"Remember," her father says, with authoritarian tone, "everything that happens in a home is the woman's fault." and he continues, "Your obligation is to remain with your husband."

Tears flow from his daughter's face. She feels misunderstood, while she listens to his words.

She knows that nothing would stop her.

This is just what she was hoping not to hear but now she understands everything. This world was for the men and their dominium has reached unlimited barriers. How can she expect protection from her father, not even he supports her. Her own father defends men in an authoritarian way.

Once she talked with her father she felt rejection, but she is determined to depart immediately. She doesn't feel understand even by her father but she still is going to follow her plan.

THE INVISIBLE DOOR
Mireya Mudd

CHAPTER FOUR
Going back home

Ana Laura's flight is not available until next day and she is hiding with her baby in the Holiday Inn hotel in Moorefield. Hopefully, Ramiro won't be able to find out were she is staying.

That evening she received a phone call from her neighbors who are insistent and ask, "Are you sure of your determination with Ramiro? He already came to us and was looking for you. He was desperate and we pretended we didn't know anything."

"I am surer than ever," Ana Laura answered, "this kind of life is unbearable and I am his prisoner. Also the way he treats me is unbearable and inhuman."

Now, that Ana Laura is feeling her first drops of freedom, nobody and nothing can change this sensation. The door is open, and now it is not invisible.

She is determined to never accept this way of life again.

She still remembers her father's words which were hammering in her mind. "You have to stay with your husband, things will get better and your obligation is to remain beside Ramiro."

She contradicted him saying: "I don't think it is that easy Dad. Whether you like it or not, I am leaving. You don't have to host me if you don't want. I will see what I can do by myself."

Obviously, she was at fault since she never told her parents about her other fights with her husband, in which he mistreated her and denigrated her as a mere beast-of-burden, a human being with no rights. Left with neither will nor completeness, she is nobody and her soul has been lost in that man's life. He has absorbed her will and has taken her personality away.

Anyhow, when her father sees her determination of coming back home, he accepts and he asks. "Which is your flight number?"

After this incident Ana Laura believes her suffering is over, not without knowing it just started. She is successful in coming back to her parent's home and she knows it is not easy to be there since in reality it's not her home.

THE INVISIBLE DOOR
Mireya Mudd

Ana Laura decides to live six months with her parents. When she arrives her mother bought her a cradle for Andrés and she gives them a room at their house. Her mother had always supported her, but her mom's personality was not dominant and she always did what her father wanted.

Her parents try giving her comfort and helping her in other ways, but feels she doesn't belong there. She requires a home of her own for her and her baby.

After six months of being with her parents, Ana Laura receives a phone call from her mother-in-law, who informs her of the importance of getting together with her in-laws. (Ramiro was still in the United States). That evening, she goes to see them to see what's going on. Ana Laura is confused about her feelings and again she is becoming blind with what is happiness and new hopes come to her life, hopes of knowing that there is somebody who loves her and wants to protect her. She is blinded again.

The situation at her parent's home is difficult and living without her husband has made her realize that in reality she didn't have any school degree or occupation in order to support herself and the baby. This situation stops her of being able to move along and be able to be economically independent.

THE INVISIBLE DOOR
Mireya Mudd

CHAPTER FIVE
A convincing story

That evening Ana Laura gets together with her in-laws and they tell her, "You don't know how Ramiro has changed. He is repented for what he has done and he is dying to see you and Andrecito. You don't know how much he has missed you guys and how much he loves you."

Her mother-in-law talks hours and hours and Ana Laura just listens to indefinite excuses. She knows she is just being brainwashed for all this seems to be so strange since she has not heard from that man Ramiro for six months. Anyhow, she knows she has to continue the theatre; otherwise she would be incapable of surviving.

Ana Laura continues listening, but her thoughts are more powerful and she starts remembering all of Ramiro's abuses and how much she has been humiliated for so many years. The need of having a home wins out and she convinces herself about all what her mother-in-law is telling her. Those words are very convincing and powerful.

THE INVISIBLE DOOR
Mireya Mudd

Ana Laura feels an unlimited protection and a new hope comes to her life. Suddenly, she wants to get into that door again. A new light is guiding her to that door. However, she still has immense doubts that threaten her. She feels hopeless in her inside but, on the other hand, she needs to make a decision.

After talking with her mother-in-law for a long time she still feels skeptical, still not convinced of these words and she tells her mother-in-law: "Look, I understand my baby and I need a home and all that, but let me tell you this, I am happy to go back to Ramiro but just for our baby, because I clearly recognize that it is important for Andrecito to have a home, but for no reason will I accept again your son's abuses.

Her in-laws explains again how repentant Ramiro is and promises her that his father will talk seriously to him as soon as he comes back.

They continued talking for hours and hours and Ana Laura confirms she will do this just for Andres, (Andrecito), but she is not going to accept that Ramiro steps on her freedom again and mistreats her.

She knows she is repeating all these words just to convince herself this decision is important and needs to be taken.

"I want you to know this," she tells her in-laws, "I just want some economical security for my baby. Otherwise I would see what I could do to support us without depending on Ramiro."

Ramiro's dad says. "Don't worry, I will talk to him, and I hope he doesn't dare to contradict me. He will hear from me if he touches you again. Remember, we support you and we just want the well being of the family."

Meanwhile in Ana Laura's mind, she still has that fantasy that Ramiro still wanted her and that he will do the impossible to recover the relationship. So, she convinces herself, "I know he still loves me and everything will go back to normal, just like when we were boyfriend and girlfriend."

Once her mother-in-law sees Ana Laura is convinced, she says: "Look Ana Laura, you also have to show him how much you love him and how much you are interested in his music and his compositions, otherwise he feels no support and nobody who cares in what he does. A wife needs to support her husband in everyway. That's the only way you can keep him forever."

When Ana Laura hears these words, she doubts that this supposed change can improve a relationship, when there is so much unloving and distance. Anyhow, she understands she needs her own home desperately so that she is the one who makes the decisions in her own house without having to feel she is still under her parents wings.

Her mother-in-law continues convincing her of how repentant Ramiro is and how he is dying to see her again and live with her. Now Ana Laura is very convinced and she is anxious in getting out of her parents home. She feels some relief and all of the sudden she doesn't remember anything anymore of what happened in the past, or, at least she has erased it from her mind. She wants to feel loved and with a home of her own she feels this is the best that can happen. She is convinced that Ramiro's parents are right. She remembers her mother-in-law words. "He still loves you and misses you and Andrecito. Give him a second chance. Look, human beings can change and believe me Ana Laura, he has changed."

"We know our son has his moments of uncontrollable anger, but if you forgive a stranger of his bad actions, how can you not forgive your own husband?"

Ana Laura doesn't feel comfortable at her parent's house, and so, she decides to go back to her in-law's home. Also she believes Ramiro is regenerated and maybe he has changed his rough attitude towards her. So, saying this, she convinces herself and tells to herself. "Everything will be different, I am sure that because Ramiro has suffered so much he is going to appreciate us better and he will make an effort to keep a good relationship. All this is up to me."

Ana Laura feels a new illusion, finally she is going to be happy with Ramiro and he will understand more her feelings of developing herself as a person. A new illusion is now in her mind and now she really wants to see and hug him, support him and love him. After all she tells herself. "I

THE INVISIBLE DOOR
Mireya Mudd

believe I still love him and I am sure he can do something about his problem."

That evening, she decides to install herself in her in-laws house. She moves in with her baby to wait for Ramiro's coming and she tells her in-laws she wants to go next day to pick up Ramiro and clear any past problems and readjust their lives.

THE INVISIBLE DOOR
Mireya Mudd

CHAPTER SIX
Did she make the right decision

That morning Ana Laura wakes up frustrated. She has been thinking everything about her relationship with Ramiro all night long. Her thoughts are confused.

She knows now there is no turning back. She is already there, in her in-laws home and she feels very insecure about her decisions.

Her husband has not called all those months and she feels strange to be there with her in-laws, instead, she knows she shouldn't be there. She knows she really doesn't belong there or anywhere close. Those past six months she has been trying to support herself and the baby, earning a miserable salary and knows she needs to study in order to be more successful in life. She has been working selling *pewter* for her brother's company, and she could understand that that kind of life was not for her, neither for her son.

That morning, she showers and gets pretty very early to go with her father-in-law to the Benito Juarez airport to

THE INVISIBLE DOOR
Mireya Mudd

pick up Ramiro. However, while she is having breakfast with everyone she notices her father-in-law trying to persuade her not to go to the airport. She perceives some anxiety in the environment and listens to her father-in-law saying. "Why don't you wait here Ana Laura, so that I can talk to Ramiro first?"

Now she thinks there is something fishy. She doesn't trust his words as she used too before. What is going on here, she asks herself?

All this recent behavior on her in-laws has awakened her curiosity even more and Ana Laura is more determined to go. Something mysterious is going on and she needs to find out the truth.

She feels some anxiety of not knowing what is happening, and also she believes it is too late to repent for she is installed with her baby in their house and thinks she doesn't have any alternatives.

Suddenly she has feelings of being at the wolf's home, without any exit, neither any refuge. She hates herself for making these fast decisions and for not being assertive about anything in her life.

She feels strange, as if she doesn't belong here, but it's too late.

Anyhow, the morning of his arrival she tells her in-laws, "I believe that after not seeing Ramiro for six months, the best will be to go to the airport."

She fears seeing reality, but she has never doubted that the best in any situation is to deal with the truth, no matter how difficult it is to confront.

Feeling a lot of insecurity, Ana Laura leaves Andrecito with her mother-in-law and she and her father-in-law, Alonso, depart to the airport, not without listening one thousand repeated advices from Mama Cecilia saying. "Remember Laurita, it is important that you show some interest in his music and his compositions so that way he will feel valued. That way," she continues, "Ramiro will improve his behavior toward you and he will feel more appreciated."

What's going on? Ana Laura thinks. I thought Ramiro was repented about all this and he was dying to see me and reunite with his family and now it is clear that all this has been a trick. Anyhow, she feels she still needs to see Ramiro to see how real her perception is of this new situation.

Mama Cecilia's words hammered in her head and she thinks she might be right. I am going to try so that Ramiro feels better being with me and that way I will save our family.

When they arrive to the *Benito Juarez* airport, Ana Laura can see the intense movement that's going on in that place; all the people seemed to be in a hurry from the baggage attendance carrying the luggage to the nervous crowd and people pushing each other. It is easy for Ana Laura to integrate to this agitated movement which justifies her desperate feelings, her feelings goes in tune with the agitation of the place and she matches the natural rhythm of that place, her heart beats accelerated.

All of the sudden, Ana Laura encounters a confused environment, very accelerated and her nervous stage increases even more. The tempo of the place goes with the

THE INVISIBLE DOOR
Mireya Mudd

rhythm of the passengers which are coming from different places. Dad Alonso and she are standing in the waiting room. He is joking as always, with his nice, kind temperament.

They start seeing passengers from United Airlines flight #1021, her heart is pounding and very accelerated for she knows Ramiro will show at any time and she is unclear of what to do, how to behave, what to say. Her throat is blocked, and at the same time her heart is pounding with irregular beats. She feels an unnatural situation and she doesn't feel comfortable at all.

Suddenly she sees Ramiro. He has left his hair grow as a hippie and his appearance is dirty but the woman in her still has the idea that everything will be solved.

She feels some kind of excitement and she waves her hand so that he sees her, but he seems to be distracted, acts superior, indifferent and he is not aware of where his father and wife are located.

Ana Laura sees suddenly Ramiro is approaching his father and greets him, but reacts superior with her. He seems to be cold and indifferent and does not react to her presence.

Now Ana Laura doesn't know what to do. Her thoughts are blocked and she asks herself "What's going on here?" She doesn't understand anything and feels hurt and angry. At the same time she sees everything clearly that she has been manipulated so that Ramiro and she get reconciled. Apparently he has been manipulated too.

On the way back to her in-laws home a dialogue is going on, just between Ramiro and his father. She feels excluded like she doesn't even exist. She sees her in-law effort to include her in the conversation, but is impossible since Ramiro makes it very clear that he has decided not to talk to her.

Ana Laura wants to make conversation with the men but she feels rejected severely and also ignored and now she is trapped in a tangled arrangement with no exit. Her immaturity has stopped her from talking how she is feeling, and experiences feelings of rejection and not being liked. In her immature mind she still thinks she can change the situation with her husband, but inside she does not know how such a fact can tolerate more being unloved and indifference.

That evening Ana Laura felt used only as a sexual object, without love, no understanding, much coldness, deprecated and humiliated by this man calling himself her husband. He had practically commanded her to give him sex. He had not communicated with her during the day and now he was ordering her around like a prostitute, humiliating her and showing her who was in charge in their relationship.

The woman in Ana saw a man who did not want to talk to her and treated her like an object of ownership. Now, she doesn't know who she is anymore. Her feelings are of death, all her body is numbed, a body that doesn't belong to her, the one that can be utilized and humiliated at the will of her torturer. Ana Laura is now immune to pain and everything else. She doesn't want to see and feel anything around her. She doesn't feel the emotion of being alive, the

THE INVISIBLE DOOR
Mireya Mudd

woman is nobody and nothing, doesn't want to think anymore.

She knows she should have stayed with her parents before allowing this, but now is too late.

What a humiliation.

THE INVISIBLE DOOR
Mireya Mudd

CHAPTER SEVEN
Back in the cycle of abuse

It is next day after Ramiro's arrival and Ana Laura comes crying down to the house library. She wipes her tears when she hears Ramiro and his brother Alvaro talking. Alvaro is asking questions to his brother about his work. "Tell me about your compositions Ramiro, how is it going? What type of music is it?"

Ana Laura with her stupid naiveté's thinks, maybe Ramiro is hurt and needs somebody who shows interest in what he is doing. She knows this is the ideal moment to start real communication. Maybe her husband still loves her after all. She tries to talk to him remembering her mother in-law's words. "Make him feel how important is his music and show some interest in his work."

Ana Laura approaches her husband saying. "Yes, Ramiro, tell us all about everything. We want to know about your compositions."

A big silence comes from Ramiro. He does not acknowledge her or at least pretends he is not listening. He doesn't answer her question but continues talking to his brother.

He acts aloof and one more time he is hurting her. She feels an immense craving to cry but controls herself; she doesn't want to concede to the macho man's triumph. Ana Laura knows now his sadism is unlimited, now everything in their lives is growing worse.

She turns around and approaches the bookcase behind them and wipes her tears while she listens to Alvaro talking to Ramiro. "Look, if you don't want to answer Ana Laura, I am not interested in anything of your life, neither to your music," and very angrily his brother turns around and leaves the room.

Now Ana Laura is crying inconsolably. She cannot say a word and following his brother's steps, she hurries to walk out of the room. She feels humiliated and hurt and knows she doesn't belong there anymore. She is in the wrong place, in the wolf's cave and there is not exit anymore. Her inexperience in life has stopped her from talking out her situation. She feels imprisoned and in a

THE INVISIBLE DOOR
Mireya Mudd

maze with no exit. She has come freely to her executioner,

now, she just needs to conform.

THE INVISIBLE DOOR
Mireya Mudd

CHAPTER EIGHT
Too many years later

Ana Laura has let years pass her by, a life filled with turbulence, threats and mistreatments. It has been many wasted years in which reconciliation after reconciliation with Ramiro have occurred, followed by abusive incidents followed by manipulation after manipulation from his parents.

Ana Laura feels incapable of doing anything, without a career to protect herself, without money or a position in her home, and more than anything she knows Mexican society protects the macho men showy attitudes. Men are protected no matter what they do. She is now hit by a deep depression where everything is difficult to do from getting up and taking her child to school, to do the home chores and more than anything to develop herself as a person.

Everyday, the woman in her makes a big effort to continue showing a good example to her son and to teach him all she is capable of doing and trying to avoid thinking of her unstable home environment.

THE INVISIBLE DOOR
Mireya Mudd

When Andrés turned three years old in 1981, Rodrigo, her second son, is born in Mexico City and Ana Laura feels a new renaissance, a new illusion. Andrés won't be alone anymore and he will have a companion and playmate. She is again happy. Her happiness is immense, but it doesn't last long because she has contradictory illusions. She believed now that there was a second baby in the family, Ramiro would change and would be more understanding, caring and loving. Ana Laura was mistaken one more time, since he continued to be the same and now even more apprehensive and strict with the wellbeing of both kids. She remembers how at all times he wants to know if she takes good care of them, if she feeds them properly. There is no trust on his part and her life continues to be miserable.

Now, as if that wasn't enough, her mother-in-law, Carolina, visits Ana Laura everyday, showing up at their home for any excuse and trying to control her home. Ana Laura is now controlled by two persons instead of one.

Her mother-in-law wants to be involved in everything, checks if the baby has a rash, changes him and wants to supervise everything that happens.

Ana Laura considers herself very responsible but to be watched and controlled by two people, she feels insulted with so many observations. She has always been very independent and she doesn't want this intrusion and she won't allow it for this is a complete abuse of her individuality.

It was a relief the day when Ramiro told her. "We are leaving for Taxco and we will be living at the new home that my parents built in Marfil."

"But, isn't that the house they built to spend time together during the weekends?" Ana Laura asked.

"Yes, but they are offering it to us and also I am getting a new job at the Main Theater, so get started and have everything ready by the end of this month."

"And your job as a dentist?" she asked.

Earlier, Ramiro had sold all his equipment and two dental offices because his real vocation was to be a musician.

THE INVISIBLE DOOR
Mireya Mudd

"Let's forget about that," said Ramiro, "I was not born to be a dentist."

Listening to those words, Ana Laura knows that living off income from being just a musician is very difficult, but she feels a new renaissance to her liberation and she doesn't have any other remedy than to accept. She knows her word in her family is soundless, and now she will only need to deal with her husbands temper. This situation was not very inspiring but at least Carolina wouldn't be intruding so much anymore.

THE INVISIBLE DOOR
Mireya Mudd

CHAPTER NINE
A new home

Just a few months after Rodrigo was born they moved to Taxco. For Ana Laura her children were a blessing and that compensated for the difficulties and fights with her husband.

She and her family were going to arrive to that beautiful, brand new home that her in-laws built in the best part of town. The in-laws would come to visit sometimes but the home was Ana Laura's new permanent residence. It was a colonial new house, a huge house with five stories, a yard and a basement with a wine cellar to receive their guests.

Ana Laura was very happy and she was hoping to be able to study in Taxco, since it was a smaller city.

Before, when Andres was a baby, they had lived in the little town of Taxco but in a smaller house, in a part of town full of students and many possibilities and facilities to study. It was there that Ana Laura studied one year of literature at the university and also took contemporary dance classes at the local theater.

Sadly, she was fooling herself since things went well just temporarily for her destiny was already traced in stone. Happiness was just for a brief moment. Once arriving at Taxco, her problems with Ramiro started over again. A happy life was only a dream and reality was back. Her abusive problems came back quickly when they started life in Taxco.

When Rodrigo started going to school, Ana Laura started teaching English as a Second Language (ESL), in the town. This created a lot of agitation with Ramiro since he wanted her to stay home and do house chores. She was doing seven classes a day to be able to deal with her solitude. Everything in her marriage was going from bad to worse. Confrontations and agitations grew day by day. Now Ana Laura, more then ever, could see the big mistake she had made coming back to that man and her life was full of anguish and desolation. How could she have been such a fool and believe that everything would be different? Ramiro was still the same abusive man and now that he had accomplished what he wanted, he felt more powerful to make her do what he wanted her to do. How did she allow him to depersonalize and minimize her to such a degree where her opinion and will did not count at all? Where she had become merely an object and the only will that counted in her house was his. How could she have accepted so much trampling and mistreatment?

More then ever, she knew it was not only Ramiro's fault but hers as well. It was she who allowed all that abuse to happen.

Many years passed and finally she was able to understand that when someone is victimized it is because he or she has not put-up any resistance. Because of that weakness, for having feelings of not being able to confront life and situations causing low self-esteem, a thousand other reasons show up which are incomprehensible to the one who allowed somebody to victimize or be victimized.

When Ana Laura realizes this fact, she decides to get a divorce after sixteen years of being married. Only then could she feel free. But her feeling of liberty is not going to

THE INVISIBLE DOOR
Mireya Mudd

last long for in a short time she sees her freedom is only

faked.

THE INVISIBLE DOOR
Mireya Mudd

CHAPTER TEN
Yet an incomplete life

Even after her divorce from Ramiro, Ana Laura is still under the yoke of her executioner who controls all her movements. He moved into the little house on the next yard and is vigilant to every movement she does and everyday he is there to watch her. She asks herself, is this freedom?

Everyday Ramiro keeps harassing her. He calls her everyday and keeps controlling her life. Ana Laura's life continues being a hell on earth.

* * *

To keep her mental health, Ana Laura reads Paul's letters with passion (her American boyfriend). She reads them often without missing any detail, and she rereads them to feed her soul and feel protected and loved.

The irony is that before Ana Laura and Ramiro got divorced, he introduced Paul to Ana Laura in an art gallery where they were exhibiting art work by John Nevin and other famous Guanajuato's painters.

THE INVISIBLE DOOR
Mireya Mudd

Once she and Paul met, they were attracted immediately and a strong love between them started from that first night.

Ana Laura and Paul had a lot in common and they talked that first night for many hours. They were very compatible and Paul was very sensitive about the difficult situation and the yoke which Ana Laura lived under and her resolution of getting a divorce from that man who had subjugated her for so long.

One year passed by in which Paul and Ana Laura wrote to each other everyday and the next summer Paul decided to go and visit her in Taxco, where she lived.

After one year of her divorce from Ramiro, Ana Laura and Paul were very much in love and Paul decided to talk to Ramiro.

Ramiro was in a rage after hearing the news about Ana Laura wanting to leave with Paul and their two children and go to the United States.

That evening Paul arrived at their home to talk to Ramiro and the kids. The expression in Ramiro's face was of much anger and uncertainty.

Ana Laura wanted to be successful in taking her children with her and Paul, since they were twelve and fifteen years old and she had raised them all their life. In reality they needed her more than Ramiro. All her hopes were to take them with her and have a happy and peaceful life with Paul.

That evening Ramiro came down from the top floor when Paul arrived to talk to him. Paul greeted him and they started to talk.

"Hi, Ramiro," Paul says nervously.

Ramiro with a sour tone talks to Paul about music and literature, but it is noticeable that he is not his friend anymore. After a few minutes Ramiro interrupts Paul asking, "Well, and now tell me why you are visiting me?"

Continuing, Ramiro answers his own question. "I already know why you are here since Ana Laura has briefed me on some of the purpose of your visit."

Paul, somewhat nervous introduces the subject saying. "As you must know, Ana Laura and I are in love and we would like to get married and live together, but, on the other hand you know Ana Laura loves her children immensely and she wants to take them with her. Otherwise it will be very difficult for her and for them to be separated."

"I know very well that you travel a lot to Mexico City to take care of your other job and you wouldn't be able to take care of them as they need, so I propose you let them go with their mother."

Making a pause, Paul continued, "I hope you can understand that she needs to go since she cannot stay here. Her mental health is deteriorating under so much tension. She has the right to develop as a person, to study and to also be successful in the world of work."

While Paul is saying this Ana Laura observes Ramiro and she can see his fury building in his face. She knows he can be very vengeful and violent, so she fears the worst.

Suddenly her thoughts are interrupted by Ramiro's words. "This is something we can look into," he answers irritated. "One thing is that Ana Laura wants to go, but my children, we will see. They have to decide for themselves." Saying this, without wanting to listen anymore to Paul's words, he gets up and calls the children. "Come here, we have to talk, but privately," and saying this he walks fast with them to the top floor of the house where nobody could listen to them.

Ana Laura is very concerned and aggravated and knows it is not going to be easy. She knows she needs to intervene immediately, so she follows them all the way to the top of the house. "Excuse me Ramiro, but I need to listen to them too."

Ramiro blocks her way to continue getting inside of the room where her two children are waiting terrified and he says. "Excuse me bitch, this is only between me and my children," and after saying this, he closes the door leaving her on the other side of the door and stopping her from coming into the room.

After knocking over and over on the door, her efforts to get inside are useless. She rushes down to Paul crying. "He is not allowing me inside to be there and talk to them. He is going to manipulate them so that they don't go with us." Crying, she is holding Paul with uncontrollable shaking and frustration. Paul is holding her with a lot of love and he expresses." Don't worry; he will opt on giving them to you. You will see. Generally, the male parent does not want to take care of the children. Please cool down, my love."

A whole hour passes and her agony is terrifying her. She can imagine the worst and knows Ramiro would fight until the end with no limit to convince them that this is his only resource to make her stay.

Suddenly they see Ramiro coming down looking pale walking beside the children. They were also pale looking.

Ana Laura is sure they will go with her. "Well, Ramiro says, I have talked to them and now they will decide who they want to stay with," and he asked them.

"What do you think, my kids? Who do you want to go with?"

The woman cannot understand why Ramiro is telling all this in a natural way, and cannot see the delicate situation and he cannot see farther than his wishes of triumph.

THE INVISIBLE DOOR
Mireya Mudd

They are mute and their faces are now red.

"Come on kids," Ramiro continues, "tell her, who are you staying with?"

She feels anger and frustration. The woman knows that because of Ramiro's strong personality, her children can be easily manipulated and can push them to decide something that in reality they don't want.

Andrés answers first. "With you, Dad," and right after Rodrigo says. "Well…

"Come on, tell her," the father forces him.

Under pressure Rodrigo says. "Well, I want to be close to my friends and want to stay here also."

Ana Laura felt like a bucket full of cold water had fallen on her. She could not go back on the decision to go to America. Her past life has been miserable and she was on the borderline of going crazy. She knew for her mental wellbeing she did not have any other option than to leave.

The door is not invisible anymore but all these decisions will bring consequences and leaving her children behind is out of her capabilities. Now she felt helpless, without strength to continue her way, trapped in a labyrinth without an exit.

How can she enjoy Paul's love faraway from her children? That was not on her plans and now she feels her happiness disrupted. She is feeling incomplete and hopeless.

All of a sudden she hears Ramiro's words of triumph:

"How is that? Mother f…..? You'll leave but without them because my children stay with me!" Ramiro is grinning as he repeats, "How is that?"

She listens to his winning bantering and her face is full of tears and uncontrollable thoughts of fear are invading her. She knows there is nothing she can do with Ramiro's strong manipulation over the children. They have been brainwashed and one more time he was commanding over their will, thinking that that will be enough for her to not leave.

Ramiro really thinks she is not leaving. For Ana Laura, it is not that easy but it is time to emancipate herself, liberate herself and more than anything heal mentally of all the many aggressions and mistreatments.

She knows she is leaving her heart with her kids and her happiness will be curtailed forever for not having them with her.

That night Ana Laura makes the decision and the resolution of leaving. Her strength is weakening and her mental health is deteriorating. She cannot continue the battle; nobody could understand more than her of what she is passing through and why she is making this determination. She knows if she stays she will be controlled, stepped on and manipulated the rest of her life. It is a very-very difficult step but necessary for her wellbeing.

THE INVISIBLE DOOR
Mireya Mudd

Chapter 11
A healing heart broken again

Many years have passed for Ana Laura to try and mend her health and wounds. Her soul was not complete and her hurt was left unhealed since she did not have her children's company and love close at hand. Paul's constant company and serenity helped begin restoring her health and patch up her wounds but life was taking a turn for the worse.

Things started to be different as Paul's strong love was deteriorating. They had lived eight years together and now she heard Paul using hurtful words towards her. Those words made her wonder if the sacrifice of not being with her children and family was worth the separation.

Ana Laura felt totally fragile, vulnerable and hurt in her second marriage. Paul was the total opposite of Ramiro, very liberal in his personal control but could not offer much in the way of financial security. He was treating her like he suddenly didn't trust her, like she was a robber.

What's going on with these men with whom she doesn't feel protection? Her second marriage was breaking up. She remembers how much love joined her and Paul and she does not want to throw everything away. He is the one who freed her and her gratitude and love are immense, but now Ana Laura is starting to feel the old feelings of being humiliated, of not having support and of being totally unprotected.

Paul is comparing her with her dad's wife, his stepmother. Ana Laura doesn't have any words to express the anger and the immense sadness that is penetrating her heart like a sword.

Maybe he is not a man to be married forever and she thinks at this point he is not going to stay the same as when they first met. Paul is unique and marvelous, full of qualities and she knows of those good qualities even though he is saying those hurtful words. She believes he just wants her to become independent, and that's his only purpose.

That persistent thought in her mind makes her remember how Paul wanted to amend what he had said during that trip to Canada.

THE INVISIBLE DOOR
Mireya Mudd

He was repentant of what he said that morning and arriving to Canada he was trying to restate his words. But, it was too late for she had been crying for most of their trip to Canada.

When they stopped to eat at Wendy's, Paul testified openly in front of his son, Tom, how his retirement money would be distributed equally between his children and her. Suddenly, when Paul saw her crying, not because of the money situation but for his distrust towards her, he tried to correct the damage of his words. What was hurting her most was Paul's unfair words which began to weaken their relationship.

Ana Laura was mute and immersed in her own thoughts.

And now he wanted to remediate the damage he had done, she thought. It was too late, the damage was irreversible.

She understood that when one hurts another person it is almost impossible to remediate the situation. She was thinking about the falseness of eternal love in which many couples live, of false hopes which almost every new couple has at the beginning of a relationship and later on becomes problematic and sometimes irresolvable.

Now she was comparing her new live with her past life. At least Paul was sincere and was not faking what other couples will do in this situation, when they know there is no love anymore but continued a fictitious life just for appearances.

Ana Laura is profoundly affected. She knows her relationship with Paul has deteriorated and now is almost impossible to heal.

There is a big contrast between the two men with whom she had lived. Both of them were opposites, one possessive and the other liberal, one aggressive and the other relaxed, one dominant and the other shared his thoughts and encouraged the development of the other person. What both of them had in common was both are artists, creators and both needed lots of space to create.

Ana Laura was thinking. "Why have I always chosen the same kind of men, creative men?"

THE INVISIBLE DOOR
Mireya Mudd

Without thinking much she knows the answer. When she was little she used to spend a lot of hours analyzing life, sitting under the water tank at the top of her house, (the only refuge to have some solitude between so many brothers and sisters). She always found solitude as her companion, and she needed many hours of contemplation and meditation, without thinking much, she knew the answer. Her brother's were the ones who gave her the space she needed and somehow she also liked to create and write. That's why she accepted those men.

Ana Laura submerged in her own thoughts was apparently listening to Paul's words, but at that instant she was in her own thoughts. He was continuing to explain his position, but now, she knew she would never again depend on any man. Something was broken.

She finally realized that women are unprotected when they completely depend on a man and it is very important to get independent economically and emotionally.

CHAPTER TWELVE
Distrusted and offended

Ana Laura has conflicting feelings by the Kincardine's streets in Canada, close to Paul's cottage beside Lake Huron.

She knows she is running away from herself. It seems almost impossible to stay in one place. She just finished arguing with Paul and she has told him how offended she feels to have compared her with his stepmother.

He answered. "I just want to make sure that this money is going to be for my children."

Feeling insulted Ana Laura says. "Don't you know I left another man who had much more money than you, even though with you, I lived with a sincere love and respect to my individuality?"

Paul interrupts, telling her that one third of the inheritance is going to be for her. She is perplexed and says. "Don't you understand? I will never feel the same for you anymore, to live with a stranger who doesn't trust me?"

THE INVISIBLE DOOR
Mireya Mudd

"It's the fact, not the money," she insisted. She cannot listen anymore and leaves in a rush out of the cottage, after grabbing her purse and the keys to the car. Paul hinders her going, asking. "Where are you going?"

"I am going to Kincardine's" she replies. When she gets in the car she still hears Paul shouting. "Remember, if you are planning to leave don't come back on the days your children are coming. Take them to a hotel in Toronto and pay for it but don't bring them to my cottage."

"I will make sure that we'll remain in Toronto," she says in a tone of indignation.

Driving through Kincardine's streets, she knows she is in another step of her life. She needs to start planning a new future where she shouldn't depend on Paul or anybody.

She starts remembering a conversation she had with her dad before when she visited in Mexico. She had glorified and admired Paul telling her parents. "He is a very good man, goodhearted and intelligent." And her dad answered. "All men are the same, just men."

THE INVISIBLE DOOR
Mireya Mudd

What did he mean? She has asked herself. And now everything was falling into place.

She continued walking in Kincardine's. Her eyes full of tears, wandering with no route, without daring to come back. She feels the wound is now open.

Back to July 18, 1999

That evening Paul, Tom and Ana Laura were heading to the Johnson's on Bruce Beach. They had taken whiskey and gin. Ana Laura remembers the conversation she had with Paul that evening while they were heading to that house beside the lake and admiring the landscape and the sunset.

Paul was saying. "In order for a woman to obtain her real freedom, she needs to become independent and the only way of doing this is when the man withdraws his protection from her."

He continued saying that that's why his intention was not to inherit anything and reminding her. "You will have a third part of my inheritance since you are still unable to support yourself. That's the only way of becoming mature and being a complete individual."

Paul continues talking but her understanding is disconnected.

Once Ana Laura rejects what Paul has offered, she tries to explain how in the Latino culture men never leave their women financially unprotected.

Again seeing that Paul does not understand what she is trying to explain, the feelings of being offended, rancor and anger comes back and her tears have betrayed her again. She knows both of them come from different cultures but for a Latino woman Paul's attitude is incomprehensible.

Feeling herself gaining strength she hides her feelings to show her husband, Paul, she is strong and that his words will not affect her.

Suddenly she says. "You are right, now I see everything clearly."

"What do you mean?" Paul asked nervously.

THE INVISIBLE DOOR
Mireya Mudd

"What I am saying is that now I can see more toward my future and if this is the situation, its better I start looking for myself." Then she continues, "I won't need to have you beside me," she said without thinking but with the firm hope of hurting Paul.

Paul, trying to remain strong said. "You know that I have never interfered in your personal development, so do what you have to do and stop seeing me as interfering. Take all the necessary roads to reach your objectives."

That afternoon with a beautiful sunset Ana Laura remained mute and her thoughts invaded and blocked her own words. It was so difficult to be raised with hopes and expectations and suddenly be submerged in a totally different world than the one she lived before, where the culture was totally different and there was no protection on her husband's part.

Anyhow, she knows she is seeing herself as a victim and she certainly knows she needs to stop those ominous thoughts which make her feel sorry for herself. She needs to overcome these feelings and start seeing herself as a complete individual who shouldn't depend on anyone.

Some days passed by and she reads something about *Logo therapy,* where this science teaches the human-being how to develop completely as a person and mainly tells the individual how not to have any expectations from anybody to survive. She doesn't want to fall in the roll of a victim. Ana Laura needs to be able to become a complete person without needing to depend on another to survive. Now all this is very clear.

She knows she needs to depend only on herself and needs to be able to continue ahead. With her second husband she was able to study in college and later she took a masters program in Latin-American Literature. It is now that she is remembering Paul's inspiring words which said she needed to study even if she was thirty eight years old. Ana Laura felt she was too old and was debating this and he had contradicted her saying. "You can become thirty eight years old with a masters degree or without it, so you decide." What would she have done without him? It's like

God put him in her way, just when she needed him the most.

Paul had always been her inspiration and she is still in denial about losing her marriage. She is blinded by her complete veneration towards Paul.

That day Ana Laura had a rebirth of feelings. Feeling a sense of comfort, she knew from now on she could depend only on herself. She felt a need to tell the world what she had learned, her knowledge about life, to prove what she was able to do by herself. She needed to find new goals. She might need to go to a more sophisticated town where she could develop her full capacity, earn more money and not depend on anyone.

Yes, that day and into the evening she could see everything more clearly.

*　*　*

The Latino man protects the woman in order to enslave her and he gives her a home and food in exchange for submitting to domination. Holding her back to develop intellectually, he doesn't want her to excel more than him and he does this in a very subtle way where she feels protected and secure. Instead, the woman needs to be an excellent cook, lover and host for gatherings of people that the husband brings home.

The Latino woman cannot make any claims, nor develop as a complete and independent person.

The Latino woman creates a dependency on the man and in exchange he obtains an expert in socializing, in home chores and childcare, but inept in her own development and incapable of becoming independent.

* * *

Now Ana Laura feels better and believes God has put her in this life of suffering for some reason and now she is starting to understand everything. It was a jumble of issues which defined itself. An immense calm and confidence comes over Ana Laura and all of a sudden she feels capable of overcoming any adversity.

In Ana Laura's mind she remembers some last episodes with Paul where they were starting to fight and contradict each other. But also, she could still remember the good

THE INVISIBLE DOOR
Mireya Mudd

parts of her relationship with Paul, all those adventures she had with him. It was something so special and so full of life.

THE INVISIBLE DOOR
Mireya Mudd

CHAPTER THIRTEEN
A walk in the park

All that happened with Paul is very different than what happened before in Ana Laura's life with her first husband, Ramiro.

And so she remembers those final days with Paul. It was one of those days in which Ana Laura was feeling extremely tired after working all day long attending to customers at the restaurant in her little town of Petersburg.

When she arrived home she just wanted to relax and rest, but she could not expect everyone to feel the same way. She was hoping she just could take her shoes off and relax. Her husband Paul wanted to walk in Seneca Rocks.

Paul is impatient, waiting for her arrival and while she is taking her shoes off, he stops her from doing this saying. "Don't take your shoes off. We have to walk."

"What are you saying? We have to what….? I am very tired. I worked all day on my feet. Let's stay at home my love. I can prepare a good dinner and we can sit close to the fireplace and read."

THE INVISIBLE DOOR
Mireya Mudd

"Don't be lazy" Paul insisted, it will be a sin to stay at home with this fascinating afternoon. Remember, today the spring starts and we have to take advantage of these days full of light."

Ana Laura thinks for a while. She wants to please him so she decides to go. It didn't take long to feel happy about that marvelous idea for she adores Paul's creativity and spontaneity.

She puts her tennis shoes on, slips into a sweatshirt and covers her head with a big sombrero. While they go out of the house in a hurry, they grab a pair of oranges. Sometimes, she thinks, Paul wants to hike for many hours and they might be thirsty, so that is a good idea.

While traveling for thirty seven miles towards Seneca Rocks, Paul is happy. He adores nature and he is singing, "There is no cure for love," by Leonard Cohen. She is enjoying the landscape, the colorful flowers in the mountain, the trees, and the reddish sky which reminds her of Velasco's paintings. She is now very happy for coming. What a great idea.

THE INVISIBLE DOOR
Mireya Mudd

Finally they arrive and start walking in the mountains. The fresh air and exercise reinvigorates her energy. What a gorgeous landscape and so close to their home, how awful to go back to the city. Close to six o'clock, Ana Laura notices the sun getting low on the horizon. It will be a spectacular sight on top of the mountain.

Somebody left a t-shirt beside a big rock near the river while they were hiking up and Paul asks. "I wonder whose it is?"

They continue walking through many hills and Ana Laura asks Paul if he didn't think it was a little late to hike all the way to the top, since it was getting dark.

"We have enough time to arrive all the way to the top." He answers with a secure tone.

The last 10 yards were the hardest since they were crawling through the rocks to reach the peak in order to see the valley and the sunset at Seneca Rocks.

Ana Laura thought. How boring it would have been to remain at home. What a marvelous idea, so very creative and she likes adventures.

THE INVISIBLE DOOR
Mireya Mudd

So, Ana Laura expressed her feelings and tells Paul. "People don't enjoy nature anymore. People prefer to stay at home and watch television. They have lost contact with nature, the real enjoyment of life."

"It's true," Paul answered, "Who would change this sunset for the booboo tube? People have artificial lives. Look how….."

Ana Laura interrupts him suddenly saying. "Let's go, it's getting dark."

"I hate it when you interrupt me when I am half way through talking."

"Don't be so sensitive," she said smiling, "I was listening to your words but what if we don't have time to go back with some light? Let's go, please."

"Trust me, Paul insists, I have been walking through these mountains all my life, and I know perfectly how much time we have left."

"Sit down and enjoy the sunset. We don't have many opportunities to watch this. There is plenty of time until it gets dark."

THE INVISIBLE DOOR
Mireya Mudd

She decides to trust Paul since he has much more experience in the woods.

Soon she sees lights shining out from some of the little houses on the horizon.

Ana Laura starts to get nervous. Something is telling her they should be on their way back.

I might need to tell him again, she thinks. No, I shouldn't, she answers to herself. He might think I am obsessed.

Finally he proposes they begin the departure back home.

What a relief, she thinks.

Walking down the mountain, Ana Laura is enjoying the forest and the trees, listening to the variation of sounds, sometimes difficult to differentiate. "What is that sound?" she asks.

"It's an owl." Paul answers, "Don't you love it?" It's my favorite sound. They only sing at night."

Paul continues talking while he accelerates his walking. "Alright, it's getting dark, so we better speed up."

THE INVISIBLE DOOR
Mireya Mudd

Ana Laura starts to get mad, now she knows they should have started back much earlier. It is not even worth it to mention it but better to concentrate on getting back ASAP.

She starts walking as fast as she can but Paul is getting much ahead of her.

"Wait," she shouts, now with some anxiety, "Can't you understand I worked all day? I cannot go much faster."

He shouts back angrily. "We could have had enough time to get down the mountain if it wasn't because you were going so slowly. It will be your fault if we don't arrive before dark."

She is furious and now he is making her the fault for the stupid resolutions that he has taken.

Finally when darkness had fallen there was neither moon nor stars to illuminate the path as Paul waited for her.

While Ana Laura walks fast down the mountain, she can hear her own heart beating. The darkness is coming fast and the road is almost impossible to see. The darkness is absolute. She tries to remain calm before her fears and

THE INVISIBLE DOOR
Mireya Mudd

concentrate on walking faster.

Now, she can hardly see anything, not even their shadows. It is total darkness.

All of a sudden she crashes against some trees. She needs to touch a tree by tree to find her way back. Ana Laura is more frightened than angry.

She remembers how in the movie theater or in the theater one can get used to the darkness and see after a little while, so, she tells Paul. "Wait until we get used to the darkness to find a new path."

"You don't understand," answers Paul angrily, "this is not like the movie theater for this is complete darkness."

She has never been so scared in her whole life. She remembers her dad who taught her to be strong in any situation, and how to confront any difficulty in life, so she tells Paul. "Give me your hand, we will find our way."

Soon they were tripping over tree roots, rocks, trees and unknown objects.

"How can you do this to me?" Ana Laura screams angrily, "I thought you knew what you were doing."

THE INVISIBLE DOOR
Mireya Mudd

"Shut up." Paul answers in anger

Let's sit here, she suggests and wait until the light comes back in the morning. We will never find our way in this darkness.

She starts crying in an underhanded way. Now her strength has been betrayed by her tears but her father had taught her to be brave during a crisis. While both were in control of their emotions everything would be fine.

Ana Laura was wondering if Paul was scared too and she asks. "Do you know where we are now?"

"There is a path up ahead which divides two ways," Paul says, "but right now I cannot find the division."

"What will happen if you don't find it?"

"Then we will need to spend a night in the forest. How about that?" Paul says with a mocking tone.

"This is your entire fault," Ana Laura says reproachfully, trying to not cry. "I told you we should have started much earlier."

"I had forgotten how slowly you walk;" Paul snapped at her, "If I was alone I would already be there."

THE INVISIBLE DOOR
Mireya Mudd

"Next time you can hike by yourself." She answers sarcastically.

All of a sudden, Ana Laura screams, "Come here Paul, I fell in a hole, help me, and hurry up, please." Paul comes back in a hurry and falls in the same hole. Pretty soon both were laughing off the funny situation.

Paul, holding her says; "Listen my love, even tough we might need to spend the night here, it's not the end of the world. It's not cold, and we will not freeze."

Ana Laura sees yellow eyes staring at her and screams. "What is that?"

"Where?" Paul asked.

"Those eyes?"

"It's your imagination, let's keep walking."

Ana Laura insists; "I saw those eyes."

"I saw those yellow eyes," Ana Laura insists.

"It might have been an owl." Paul says.

Now they are walking and using their feet as eyes, without knowing which direction to take.

"Can you hear something?" Ana Laura mentions.

"Now what," answers Paul, again angry.

"Listen."

"For goodness sake, it's the river. That means we're close to the bottom of the mountain, but we still need to find the bridge."

Ana Laura sees some reflective object close to her feet, something white. She reaches for it and says. "Look, it's the white T-shirt."

Paul, showing some relief says. "This T-shirt tells us exactly where we are."

Both of them felt an immense relief when they crossed the wooden cracking bridge. They never felt so happy at seeing their car waiting for them.

How comfortable and warm they felt arriving back at their little country house beside the mountain and for the first time in her life Ana Laura could value the security that that home gave her in the United States.

THE INVISIBLE DOOR
Mireya Mudd

CHAPTER FOURTEEN
Old friends

So many thoughts, so many good and bad times which Paul and Ana Laura lived through together, of memories impossible to erase.

Walking through the woods of West Virginia, Ana Laura starts remembering her past with Ramiro (her first husband). It is difficult to erase those thoughts of resentment by him as she remembers what happened when she went to visit the antique town of Taxco in which she lived with her first husband.

By then she already had finished studying her career in Latin-American Literature in the United States. She had been married to Paul for several years and was teaching as a Spanish teacher in a school in West Virginia.

She was in Taxco at her favorite coffee shop *La posada,* waiting to get together with some other women that she knew from the past. By then Ana Laura had been away for three years and she was sure the women wanted to know all about her new life. Of course it was not for

THE INVISIBLE DOOR
Mireya Mudd

interest about her well being but to have something new to talk about in town.

She asked herself, "Why do I contribute and accept the gossiping of these women who said they are my friends?"

On second thought, she thinks the get-together might be necessary since it has been a very long summer and she was yearning to have some company. Perhaps the reunion with the women will give her comfort since she sees her children so little and maybe the ladies know something about them.

Her new marriage had made her feel lonesome and not in a much better situation than her first marriage with the children.

She asks herself if Paul has so many good qualities, why does the feeling leave her with such emptiness? Love is very complex, she thinks, and at least Paul did not mistreat her as Ramiro used to do.

While her friends are arriving she is wondering how to lie. She knows these women haven't been able to taste freedom, to be independent and to develop as a complete

THE INVISIBLE DOOR
Mireya Mudd

person. The women have always depended on somebody, their intellectual development blocked like the Hispanic ruins haven't seen the light of day in this new world. The women have blocked their emotions so that they don't feel any pain. These women have conformed to their daily routine, including gossiping and talking about sicknesses of the people they know. Appearances are very important for them and the least that concerns them is their relationship with the man who supports them. They think it is his obligation to keep supporting them while they stay in their marriages just like they promised before the altar.

They don't want to talk much about their husbands, only talk about how well they can manipulate them in order to obtain what they want. They know they won't ever talk bad about them. Appearances are very important. These women live in a fictitious world. They wear masks to cover tears of disillusionment. They have taken the painless road and have lost all hope of exceeding as a person.

Ana Laura is in crisis now. Should she tell all that is going on in her marriage? She always liked sincerity and the truth. Should she continue the same game? How to lie? Her ex- neighbors in her old little town of Taxco have the natural jealousy of those who have felt freedom.

Suddenly her thoughts get interrupted.

"Hello, beautiful one," says Rosario, "as always you are very gorgeous. Marriage has suited you well. I can read it in your face. Happiness is in your eyes."

"Of course," Ana Laura answers. "I am thrilled at seeing my children again.

She feels awkward at being so good at covering her pains and she thinks they shouldn't know, not for any reason. After all, my children live here and I should cover appearances. So she rushes to answer. "How could I not be happy? My children are grown up now and I am so proud of them."

"Anyhow," Rosario interrupts, "I see you are a bit chubbier! It must be the American food, right? Of course, life there is much easier."

Rosario greets the others with her comment about Ana Laura. "I see she is very happy and well, I think if she

THE INVISIBLE DOOR
Mireya Mudd

gained weight don't worry. Look at me. I have changed two sizes myself since we met for the first time."

Now Ana Laura is thinking about the old saying that tells. "Consolation of many is ignorance." She continues smiling with all those suggestions and comments the women are telling her. While this conversation is happening she observes the mental development of her inquisitors and she knows they are stuck in their lives. Their life has been surrounded just by gossiping. They are empty and all that they are saying doesn't make any sense to her anymore.

Ana Laura takes a sour breakfast, lying, lying in some aspects, telling how happy she is and how she has been dedicated to study Latin-American Literature and how her marriage with Paul is perfect. She can see in her friends' faces of envy and stagnation. She can see how much they would like to be in her shoes. All of a sudden they changed the subject. They don't want to hear it anymore, too much pain for their consciousness.

THE INVISIBLE DOOR
Mireya Mudd

The rest of the breakfast she continues listening to talks about fashion, liposuctions, treatments to get thin, depilation and more than anything about other women, about this other woman did this etcetera. Anyone who does not belong to their group they destroy. Anybody who is not there is being devoured by them, especially the ones who have opted to stay at home and have an isolated life.

Suddenly Ana Laura focuses her thoughts in their conversation and listens.

"Do you believe Leticia Villapando was in a cheap motel with Alici Buendia's husband? Can you imagine? It's unbelievable. There is no more decency in this Taxco anymore."

Ana Laura interrupts asking. "Don't you think it is natural that she has found a lover? Didn't Rodolfo abandon her for another woman?"

All of them exchanged sights between them and after that comment they smiled trying to understand her liberal mind.

THE INVISIBLE DOOR
Mireya Mudd

Angélica interjects. "Imagine, being with a married man. She is nourished with bad milk. If we accept that behavior, later on, somebody will take our husbands away from us. We shouldn't allow that. Married women should get together to show Leticia that we won't allow anyone to be with another's married man."

Nevertheless, Lupe said, "you are right, this has to stop."

Now, Ana Laura was feeling isolated and with their comments she feels even worse. There is a lot of insincerity. The communication is obsolete, no one will express their real feelings and all those comments are covered with a mask as thick as their make-ups. She knows that nobody will comment on the truth about their marital life, and now, she is part of that lie.

Ana Laura decides to challenge them commenting. "Don't tell me the relationships with your husbands are still full of passion. Could you swear that your husbands are still loyal to you?"

THE INVISIBLE DOOR
Mireya Mudd

She gets interrupted by Aurora. "Come on woman. At this time, after so many years I don't care what my husband does, as long as my children and I have all what we need.

Rosario interrupts Aurora saying. "I don't care what Luis does either as long as my family is well provided. I don't care if I get controlled; after all, I do what I want under the table."

The world of control makes Ana Laura reflect and she shows confusion because her second marriage is failing and she asks herself. Why is this? She wants her freedom but at the same time she is scared of giving Paul his freedom. Now she isn't controlled by anybody, but she is trying to control him. Paul is getting tired of this situation and she would like to have the certainty that Paul is loyal to her. Ana Laura knows it is part of his past. She is projecting her feelings since her father was unfaithful to her mother by having an affair with his nurse co-worker.

Also Ramiro, her ex-husband, had been unfaithful all his married life and she didn't find out until she got divorced. It was a plot from her old town where everyone decided not to tell her and kept it a secret until the divorce was concluded.

Now they talk about this openly saying what good friends they were while they decided to keep it a secret in order to not hurt her. All these feelings of her past make her distrust the other sex.

In the past she lived in a golden cage with Ramiro, and now that that cage is opened, she doesn't want to ever go back inside but she has a big fear that is hard to explain invading her thoughts. She has much uncertainty in confronting life without anyone to back her up.

She knows she is independent today with Paul, even tough she has never been able to confirm her freedom for she is distrusting Paul.

Ana Laura knows she needs therapy to overcome all these feelings. She needs to create her own world and let the past stay in the past.

She knows how valuable is her husband, Paul, and how much she loves him and that's why she is determined to reach her objective. After reflecting for a long time, she knows she is not wearing the mask, she really loves Paul. He is her truthful love. She knows if she gives him his freedom he will love her forever and so she will, but always respecting their spaces.

A new light illuminates her path, for today that's enough thinking. Her mind is confused, agitated and fearful. She needs to rest.

She wants to be isolated from her friends and she excuses herself. "I am sorry but I have to go. My husband is waiting for me to have lunch together."

When she gets out of the restaurant she doesn't want to see Paul. She is a little bit hurt and her thoughts are mixed and confused.

She is sitting in the *Cantador Park* and starts thinking how her feelings towards Paul were when she made her first trip to the United States and they were still boyfriend and girlfriend.

Back then Ana Laura was divorced from Ramiro and she was always ready to defend and protect Paul without even thinking. She had idealized him at such a degree that

THE INVISIBLE DOOR
Mireya Mudd

she felt complete fidelity and submission and nobody, absolutely nobody had better talk bad about him. She wouldn't allow that kind of talk.

On that first trip their vacation was marvelous. Those ten days made her feel like they were bound for life. That man was her destiny. She never thought a bigger love could exist.

While she was with those thoughts, she buys some bread from an old Indian woman at the plaza and starts feeding the doves. She feels that big connection with them since they represent the symbol of freedom and that's why she protects them. While feeding them she starts remembering her trip back to Mexico after her first encounter with Paul.

She was really nervous in confronting Ramiro again. She was recently divorced and while she was talking on the phone with her children, she heard the sarcastic tone on Ramiro's voice in the background which told her nothing good was there for her to return home. She decided, however, to continue enjoying Paul's company and their

THE INVISIBLE DOOR
Mireya Mudd

vacation until that day announcing her return home to

Mexico.

THE INVISIBLE DOOR
Mireya Mudd

CHAPTER FIFTEEN
A trip back to Mexico

The landing at the Benito Juarez airport had been difficult. Ana Laura was coming back after spending a vacation with Paul.

While waiting for her luggage, she was worried about José (the taxi driver) not showing. He had worked for the family for many years but in reality he was Ramiro's driver. There was a possibility that her ex-husband had told him not to pick her up. José knew her story even more than what she wanted. He knew perfectly how violent Ramiro could be.

While coming out of customs, Ana Laura saw José, he was waving his sombrero. Good… she thought.

She was extremely tired. José approached to help her with her luggage.

"How was your trip? Did you enjoy it?"

"It was marvelous José. I have met the most marvelous, interesting and special man you can imagine. He treats me like a queen and he is very intelligent."

THE INVISIBLE DOOR
Mireya Mudd

"That's what you deserve Mrs. Ana Laura, you deserve to be treated like a queen, so I am very happy, it was about time for you to be happy."

Now the woman in her is ashamed of being so extroverted and open; just in a few words she had described something so intimate, easy to reveal in such a small town like her home town. All of the sudden she had to stop her words while she was remembering that José was Ramiro's chauffer.

In the States people are more frank and they talk more openly. She needed to remember Mexico was a country with an older culture and very different. However, she was determined to talk. José wouldn't betray her.

"I am glad Mrs. Ana Laura." José said while placing the luggage in the trunk. "It was about time for you to be happy."

She was so scared of seeing Ramiro again. Even though they were divorced; this was the first time she had gone abroad for some days. He would be furious and question her with many thoughts that weren't even of his concern anymore. Since they divorced, Ramiro had been in charge of filling her life with anxiety and had made it very difficult for her. It seemed that that man was still taking her as his possession.

José's son, who was about five years old, sat in the front seat on his daddy's lap. Pulling the wheel continuously, he was that kind of hyperactive child who couldn't stay still and could make anybody crazy. A little while ago he was hanging on his Dad's neck but José was very patient and was in absolute control of the driving situation.

"Tell me something," José asked, looking through the mirror while passing through a yellow light. "How do you think Mr. Ramiro will take all this?"

Ana Laura is repented in expressing her feelings with so much familiarity but at the same time she trusts José.

"I am sure Mr. Ramiro will understand that here starts a new story; don't you think? After all we are now divorced."

However, she didn't want to think about her ex-husband at that moment. While approaching their mansion, her stomach was having cramps and she started to have a spasm. Suddenly she felt quite indisposed. She starts to remember calling Ramiro the last night before coming back to her country to see how her children were and Ramiro had insulted her saying she was the worst mother in this world and was threatening her saying she will pay for that.

Just recently she had read that the mistreated person should show no fear towards the executioner because that can cause a disadvantage situation toward the one who feels oppressed. So, she needed to be strong and confront that situation no matter how difficult.

She felt some relief remembering she had Paul to fall back on and that gave her strength to confront any adversary.

Ana Laura looked through the taxi window contemplating the dry mountains of Taxco and was asking herself how long it would be to see Paul again. She was missing him extremely and she had just arrived. When would she see him again?

THE INVISIBLE DOOR
Mireya Mudd

She thought about the complex and difficult situation now that there were children involved. If her children were still babies, she would take them with her without even asking but now they were twelve and fifteen and this made the situation more complicated.

When Rodrigo was only a baby and Ramiro and she lived in Oregon, she had run far away from Ramiro with Rodrigo in her arms. When they were little, her children were only hers, an extension of her body. No doubt about it, where she used to go, they went.

Now they were grown up, with their own wills and more independent in their decisions.

She started to remember one more episode in her life with Rodrigo (her baby). He was very little and started to dehydrate. They took him to the English hospital in Mexico City to the emergency room. She remembers how close she approached God, more than ever. All she did was to beg him to recover Rodrigo. She was paralyzed with the thought of losing him. Her thoughts were interrupted then when Ramiro, the one who used to be her husband said. "I hope nothing happens to Rodrigo, because you are responsible for this situation. If something happens to him you will need to confront me. What have you given him? Have you poisoned him?" That man was telling her this while he was pointing his finger towards her.

How can a mother poison her own child, she thought. This man, her husband, is out of touch with reality.

Her stepmother was surprised while hearing this; "Come on Ramiro, don't blame Ana Laura. The baby will recover. You will see."

Her stepmother was trying to block Ramiro's path to Ana Laura.

Now she remembers the little moral support that she had with that man. She was desolated to see that they were going back to that place or *home* where so many confrontations and problems happened.

Home? Ha-ha-ha, no way was that home, she thought. What a laugh, so beautiful externally, the golden dream for many women but a nightmare for Ana Laura. Suddenly she thought how many hours she had spent sweeping the floors,

THE INVISIBLE DOOR
Mireya Mudd

cooking without any appreciation, taking care of her family without a crumb of gratitude. The only exception was her kids who always showed her with their sights how much they loved her. For a moment she knew how much she hated that house and more then anything she hated Ramiro who had been her tormentor for many years.

This place was another chapter of her life. She had left her love in the United States and her return here was filled with tension.

The trip back from the airport had happened very quickly. She was not ready. Coming out of the car like a zombie, she pays José for the ride and all of the sudden she is back in that house, which is not very inviting.

The dogs Rosco and Chalán come to greet her, moving their tails happily. She hears two crows on the pirul tree in the yard. She thinks one of the crows is Paul who is coming to inspire her to be strong and the other one is herself.

Ana Laura feels the tension all over her body. She is ready for whatever comes her way.

THE INVISIBLE DOOR
Mireya Mudd

She tells herself. Don't show any weakness, express security, you are not his possession anymore, remember.

She reads one more time what she had written the day before in her dairy and this fills her with strength to be able to confront the man again.

Dear Dairy

I am so sad. On the flight back to Mexico, I've been crying. It's unbearable to have Paul so far away. My soul is bleeding, my heart is empty, but my mind is full of beautiful memories and future hopes.

Who can forget those beautiful days, talking to each other, walking in the forest of West Virginia (how great it was when he simulated we where lost, I was so frightened), reading D. H. Lawrence stories, dancing at the discothèque, so much intimacy and enjoyment at the same time. I keep telling to myself it is quality that counts not quantity. You will see him soon again, but this doesn't give me much consolation.

THE INVISIBLE DOOR
Mireya Mudd

I know there is not complete happiness, and also I know my body needs him and now I am back at Ramiro's prison where I needed to learn how to survive and where I taught to be myself and not who this man wanted me to be.

Before going to the States I remembered having a conversation with my father about my problems with my ex-husband. My father had offered for me to live with my children in a little house that he owned outside of Yucatan, a little house in the middle of the jungle in the South of Mexico. My father told me. "Forget about what he gives you. He only gives you crumbs, and even if he gives you more you shouldn't accept his abuses. You shouldn't depend on him anymore, now you can support yourself. Now I know my father understands Ramiro, who has been abusing me and for the first time my father was giving me support.

On the other side my mom also supported me saying. "Don't worry about anything for at this place your babies and you will have everything you need."

THE INVISIBLE DOOR
Mireya Mudd

All this gives me a lot of consolation but I didn't want to depend on anybody and this complicates everything.

I remember telling my father. "It's not so easy, if I go to Yucatán I might stay without my children and I wouldn't be able to take that loneliness. They will hate to live in the jungle in that reconditioned house, in an abandoned and rural place which offers them nothing for stimulation.

This is what I told to my father, but inside of me I know I am making another excuse to not confront life by myself and somehow I want Paul's support to be able to continue life with my children.

Dear dairy, I need to be stronger to confront life and be completely independent and free myself from Ramiro's yoke and control of my past. The only way of doing this is to go far away, because if I stay here, he will never stop his intentions of controlling me. His control is like a disease.

But I ask myself. "What would happen if my children don't come with me?"

I would be lost...

CHAPTER SIXTEEN
Out of control

While coming into the garage in the big home in Taxco, she suddenly comes back to reality and a big emptiness possesses her.

On one side she is happy at seeing her children but again on the other side something is telling her Ramiro is going to be out of it. She can predict this.

While getting in through the main door, she doesn't hear anything. Ana Laura shouts towards the top of the ceiling saying. "I am here children. Come on down and greet me." She starts hearing her children's steps coming down, ready to greet her. All of the sudden she hears Ramiro's voice stopping them and saying. "Wait a minute, don't come down yet, I need to talk to her."

"But Dad, we want to see her."

"Get upstairs," he said, with a dictatorial voice. "You will have time to see her later."

A frightened moment invaded the atmosphere and Ana Laura wants to run away from this place. She knows something real bad is about to happen, but her love for her children is more powerful. She knows she needs to act strong and so, taking her luggage she precedes to start going up the stairs. Right there on the second floor is that angry man and is throwing fire from his eyes.

"Where do you think you are going mother f.....? Who do you think you are...come on...get out of here...do you think this is a hotel or a shelter? Since today I am taking care of the children...this is not your home anymore, so, let's go bitch...get out of here, shitty woman."

While telling this he took away the luggage from Ana Laura and threw them down the stairs. All the clothes were spilled over the floor.

Ramiro comes down precipitously and is chasing her around, grabs her by the arms and tries to push her out of the house to the street shouting. "Get out of here *cabrona*, mother f....."

Ana Laura holds herself at the door frame while the children run toward her and kiss her and hold her. Ramiro has lost the battle.

THE INVISIBLE DOOR
Mireya Mudd

This time he was not going to be able to hit her like so many other times. She is all teary and shaky and goes upstairs with her children to show them what she has bought for them. Now the situation has worsened and she knows she needs to get out of there soon if she wants to survive the aggressions from that evil man.

Several days passed by to allow Paul to visit her again in her home town. She thought it would be better for her to visit him in the United States since the situation with Ramiro has worsened. She is frightened and scared for Paul's life and her own life. Her ex-husband is in an irrational state and even more violent than ever.

Paul doesn't want to lose her and he writes in his last letter. "I know how difficult is this situation for you, but how can I stop myself from seeing my beautiful queen. I know it is dangerous to go there but the occasion is worth it and I need to see you again."

Ana Laura's nervous system was collapsing. This was a nightmare. Her energy was lowering in fighting to have a normal life. Ramiro insists in making her life miserable and

THE INVISIBLE DOOR
Mireya Mudd

more difficult every moment, putting their children in the middle of every confrontation as an excuse to supervise every movement she has with them.

THE INVISIBLE DOOR
Mireya Mudd

CHAPTER SEVENTEEN
Imprisoned

So many bad incidents have happened in that broken marriage with that man.

Ana Laura starts remembering how in one occasion Ramiro had called her saying. "Where are the kids?"

"They are all right her," she hesitates in answering.

"I want to talk to them," he ordered.

"The kids asked me to stay ten more minutes at their friends' home."

"I knew this was going to happen," Ramiro said angrily. I knew that once you left this house and we divorced you would do whatever with them."

"Come on mother f.......you have ten minutes to bring them in and I will be calling in ten minutes and if they are not at home, you will see what will happens."

Saying this, he hung-up the phone without allowing her to express her feelings.

Ana Laura takes her old rain coat hanging on the hat rack and shouts to her children saying. "Hurry up Rodrigo;

we have to go, where is your brother?"

"I don't know mom."

"How can you not know? Your father will be calling back in ten minutes and he will be furious."

The frightened Ana Laura runs towards her car, opens the car door. She cannot avoid still feeling under the control of that mean man. Driving and crying she heads towards the video store where Rodrigo thinks his brother has gone. Once there she tells him to go out and search for his brother. He comes back without him.

Rodrigo gets rapidly back in the car expressing some nervousness. Quickly, he says, "I believe he is at Pedro's home. Let's go look there."

Ana Laura knows her nerves couldn't tolerate these abrupt changes anymore. They make her feel overtired. She drives towards Pedro's house. When they arrive there, Rodrigo gets out quickly and runs towards the door, ringing the bell intensively. She knows her children are also disturbed because of the many conflicts. When Rodrigo sees his brother he starts scolding him saying. "Where have

THE INVISIBLE DOOR
Mireya Mudd

you been? Mom has been looking for you for a long time and our dad is furious. Come on, don't waste any time and hop in the car."

When arriving back to her children's home, Ana Laura takes off her old raincoat which has been for a long time her emergency suit, one she used to get out precipitously from that house on many similar occasions.

She is waiting nervously for Ramiro's phone call and when Andres is closing the garage door she sees his car. He is approaching furious and in a hurry. She is now shaking and cannot control herself.

She sees him approaching frantically shouting irrationally and totally out of control. "No more excuses from anyone to be out at this time of night and next time you need to confront me, mother f…. This is the last time I am allowing my children to be out of the house at nine at night."

Ana Laura simulating being very strong says. "Come on Ramiro, you know I have custody of the children, so, I am the one who should give the permission. And you know it would never be something unreasonable. Ten more minutes of extending permission is not much time to allow. Don't you think?"

She continues her explanation saying. "I remember you would come here only once a week and you were constantly interfering in my decisions."

Listening to these words, Ramiro explodes in anger. "First of all, even though we are divorced, I am the one who continues giving the orders here and secondly don't tell me when I can see my children *cabrona* (bad word) meaning wretch. "Remember the law allows me to come here for six months to pick anything I need and look," grabbing a toothbrush, he said, "I am coming today for this, so, tell me now how is it looking, eh? See what you can do about it, eh, eh?" as he laughs sarcastically.

A bright shining is projecting in his face. His eyes express hate, anger and irrationality. "And tomorrow," he continues, "we will see what I come from, eh, eh? How does it look? Is there anything you can do about it?"

THE INVISIBLE DOOR
Mireya Mudd

While telling this to her he follows her around wherever she is going. She starts getting nervous and turning around says. "Stop chasing me around, don't you understand that you cannot command over me anymore?"

Ramiro looking with bullets in his eyes said. "This is my house, eh? Remember it very well, the only intruder is you. I would love you to leave the house and get out of here. But remember, if you want to take the children with you, you would need to find a good home for all of you, similar to this, and for no reason I will allow that you take them to a shack. Since you don't have any money to fall back on, you will starve. Do you understand? So it's better that you straighten yourself up you whore, mother f……."

And seeing this clearly, he continued. "It will help if you take a close look to the divorce contract which says that only if you stay in this house can you take care of the children. Now, how is that? Don't be so sure woman because if you leave this home you lose them."

Ana Laura is aggravated by his strong words and she replies. "If I want I can take them anytime I want, so stop bothering me and don't threaten me. Stop controlling my life and leave me alone."

"Now I know why you are so secure, mother f......, just because you have met that *Gringo*. He's a loser, but wait until he sees the real situation for he will run away from all this and that way you will lose him as soon as he sees the reality."

"Is that what you think?" Ana Laura answered angry, "he loves me truly and treats me with complete respect, like you have never behaved with me. He knows how to respect a woman. He treats women like equals and not like another possession from the house. He is a complete man and he will support me, mark my words."

"Can't you see he's starving? He doesn't have anything to offer you. Do you think he can make you happy?"

Rapidly, Ana Laura answered. "Yes, that's what I want from a man, absolute recognition, respect and love, and he gives me all of that. And stop talking about him since you don't have any right to insult him, neither to tell me whom I should date, or whom I should see."

THE INVISIBLE DOOR
Mireya Mudd

While saying this, she feels all of Ramiro's weight on top of her, pushing her to the bed. Looking at his eyes they were armed with fire, expressing hate and a state of uncontrolled craziness. Ana Laura tried to get free of his weight, but it was impossible. She starts shouting. "Andrés, Rodrigo, come quick, quick, help me." Rodrigo comes with a scared face and with a timid voice he said. "What's going on?"

Immediately Ramiro lets her go and shouting while he is leaving he says. "Remember, today I came to get a toothbrush and tomorrow I will get some shoes, eh…eh? How about this for that's what the law stipulates. I still have four months to come as much as I want!" and saying this he slams the door showing an ironic smile and departs.

Ana Laura cries inconsolable. She thought divorcing Ramiro was going to fix the situation but now it has worsened.

She goes to the kitchen to feed the children while she is remembering Paul's last letter, advising her to get her complete independence from the man.

THE INVISIBLE DOOR
Mireya Mudd

Her concentration in doing activities is impossible. Her situation with Ramiro seems like a web without an escape.

Ana Laura is teaching English as a second language for seven hours a day in order to be able to confront her solitude. Now divorced, she has her apparent freedom, but she asks herself. "Is this really freedom? This is still a nightmare. How can I have a normal life under these conditions?"

She is reading Paul's letters over and over obsessively in order to keep her mental health, but a big void is reflected in her life which is so unnatural. She is still taking care of her children and that comforts her somewhat but the man that she loves is five thousand miles away from her. It is impossible to live out of illusions.

On the current situation, Ramiro, fearing that Ana Laura might take their children away to live in a foreign country hid the children's passports from her saying. "Don't think you can kidnap my children, they won't ever leave this house."

THE INVISIBLE DOOR
Mireya Mudd

Ana Laura feels imprisoned in that home…

CHAPTER EIGHTEEN
Never ending

Next day Ramiro comes home asking. "Where is Andrés?"

Ana Laura thinks the same story is repeating again and she starts replying to his question. "A friend of his will bring him back after his gym class."

Seeing anger in his eyes, she continues. "He will come back soon, his class is about to finish."

"I want my son now, at this precise moment." he said this with that sight that Ana Laura knows all to well, an out-of-control sight, the one she has seen so many-many times before.

"You should understand he is still in class, please be patient and wait."

"Don't you understand what an order is?" the ex-husband Ramiro said, throwing orange juice towards the woman's face.

Rodrigo, the youngest son was in the kitchen at the moment and seeing his mother dripping of orange juice all

THE INVISIBLE DOOR
Mireya Mudd

over her runs abruptly out of the kitchen, crying and not being able to contain himself.

She turned around furiously and getting out of the kitchen she is thinking she has to act strong so that this man doesn't abuse her anymore.

"You don't have any right," she says angrily with fire in her eyes, and saying that she turns around and departs towards the bathroom in her main room, locking the door behind her.

Rodrigo is crying and his mother can hear him crying inconsolable out of anger and absolute frustration.

At that moment she feels incapable of consoling him. Instead she rushes to go to the shower to clean all the orange juice off her clothes. She needs to recover herself and let those tears roll out.

While Ana Laura is showering she hears somebody jumping through the hall window that goes from the stairs to her room. It is Andrés. He just arrived and his father has pushed him through the window in order to accomplish his objective by opening the room and continuing the battle.

THE INVISIBLE DOOR
Mireya Mudd

Now Ramiro is including Andrés in his craziness. He still wants to continue his war.

She comes abruptly out of the shower wrapping herself in a towel and sitting on the bed, she listens to Ramiro's furious and astonished words. "I don't want this ever to happen again. You know you are the one responsible to control my children and it is important you keep command over them. It would be better if you try to be a good mother because my lawyer is following all your steps mother f......, and it is very possible that you will lose the children."

Ana Laura's situation everyday is getting worse and she screams at Ramiro saying. "Why don't you go and scold your new lover. Why do you have to put all your trash on me? But don't feel so good about it because pretty soon she will realize who you really are, and your life will become a hell, just as mine. I hope I won't be in this house to tell the story... And I am telling you this right now: I will be very happy since I won't be here anymore to hear your accusations."

THE INVISIBLE DOOR
Mireya Mudd

THE INVISIBLE DOOR
Mireya Mudd

CHAPTER NINTEEN
Abuse at every turn

Ana Laura's suffering always had some compensation and now Paul was visiting her with his son Tom, in Taxco. All of them will spend the summer together.

Everything happened quickly before she could suspect something.

She booked Paul and Tom in a hotel outside the city of Taxco to avoid any incidents with Ramiro.

Meanwhile Ana Laura is trying to see Paul as much as she can in her free times. She has many duties to do in the house, with the children and cooking and managing the kids plus teaching English as a second language. And more then anything she needs to deal with her ex-husband's behavior.

She still makes time to see Paul, which is the only event that maintains her having some fantasy and carefulness.

She is now perfectly happy and cannot contain her emotions. Every moment with Paul is a special experience. Everyday after dinner her children go out to play with their

THE INVISIBLE DOOR
Mireya Mudd

friends and she takes advantage of these moments. Her days in the evening are full of romanticism and adventure and all this seems like a dream.

On one occasion Ramiro kicks her out of the house after coming back from seeing Paul. Now she is on the street with no place to go to so she drives back to Paul's hotel.

Paul knows that the situation is getting worse when she sees Ana Laura driving to the hotel crying. It is close to two in the morning. "What's going on?" Paul asks nervously.

"I believe things are getting worse my love, and now Ramiro pushed me out of my home. Ramiro wants to force me to leave the kids and I won't allow that to happen."

"All this seems to be a nightmare and I am completely aggravated and tired."

She is crying non-stop and her strength is weakening.

"Don't worry my love, everything has to resolve itself. I promise you, there is no situation that lasts one hundred years. You will see that one day Ramiro will give up and will leave you alone with your children." While telling this to Ana Laura, Paul is hugging her so full of kindness and understanding: "Come on, cheer up, and cry to release your pain."

Paul's moral support is comforting, Ana Laura feels protected. Nothing that can happen now matters to her anymore. Now she feels strong to confront any adversity.

She still is worried for her children. What is going to happen to them? She knows Rodrigo had mentioned several times that if she leaves he will go with her. He could not tolerate his father's temper anymore or the way he treated her. One day Rodrigo mentioned to her. "Why doesn't my father leave and leave us alone?"

That night after listening to Paul's comforting words, she comes home stronger then ever and ready to fight until the end to get her children and take them with her.

One night as she arrives back to the house, she hears Marcelita (the maid) approaching rapidly saying. "I am glad you come Señora. There is the Señor in your bedroom and he is furious. He has been asking where you are and I told him you were with your friends, but he suspected you were with the gringuito and he became real upset. You don't know what has been going on here señora. It's very scary."

"That's all I still need to see that even though I am divorced he accepts me like I was his property."

Ana Laura is very nervous. She has pretended before the maid to be strong and courageous, but she knows something not very pleasant is waiting for her.

Ramiro receives her lying on her bed with his clothes on and when he saw her he immediately orders the kids to leave the room. "Go to your rooms," he said with an authoritarian voice, "I have to talk to your mom. These are not proper times to arrive. If this continues I will find a way to take the children away from you. Mother f......."

"Look Ramiro, I don't have to explain anything anymore to you. We are divorced and you don't have any rights over me."

The argument lasted for hours and hours and after a while, seeing that Ramiro was not leaving she seeks refugee in Rodrigo's room so that he will leave her alone.

THE INVISIBLE DOOR
Mireya Mudd

She remembers he had the obsession of never finishing an argument and she prefers to leave the battle camp. It was worthless to continue this so she decides to get protection in one of her children's rooms. Otherwise, Ramiro would have continued chasing her all over the house threatening, hurting and insulting her. At least in her children's rooms he will quit all this nonsense and leave her alone. That was the only secure place for her.

While telling this to Paul, next day, he says. "What? What else does this man want from you? All this time you are taking care of the children? If there is a dedicated and good mother it is you, I just don't understand this man."

"Don't pay any attention to him, my love. He is just hurt because I am in your life. I won't allow anything to happen to you. I am here to protect you."

"I am scared. His reactions everyday is more unpredictable and I don't want to be his prisoner forever. You should see how aggressive he was, for a moment I thought he was not going to be able to control his temper. My children got scared."

THE INVISIBLE DOOR
Mireya Mudd

"You cannot live threatened forever. We need to find a solution. "

"I know, but what?"

THE INVISIBLE DOOR
Mireya Mudd

CHAPTER TWENTY
Will the abuse ever end?

That evening Ana Laura goes out and visits her friend Blanca with Paul. Blanca asks while Paul is looking at the books in the library: "Wouldn't you like to leave with Paul?"

"Of course, but how can I leave without my children?"

"If they want they will follow you, but you cannot continue sacrificing for this man who treats you so badly all the time. Don't wait anymore," Blanca continues, "You have to take the opportunity when it comes, what are you waiting for?" (Saying this with her northern accent), "After all, one day your children will depart and it will be too late and you will be alone. You have shown the world how brave you are and you have made the decision of leaving this bad marriage. Let me tell you this Ana Laura, if I was you I wouldn't stop to think about this twice. You have Paul that loves you. What else do you want? The opportunities in life only come once, you have to take it or leave it, don't you think?"

"I know Blanca, but do you think the children will be alright with this violent man? What would become of them?"

"They can protect themselves, they are men. Men who abuse women only abuse women. Ramiro is a coward and with time you will see."

"Your children will always be yours and one day they will understand and follow you. There is no fight but the one that you don't do, Ana Laura. Don't be stupid."

Somehow Ana Laura knows Blanca is right. This is the opportunity to free herself from that man who tortures her and makes her suffer.

Ana Laura is in a stage of anxiety and anguishes and doesn't know what to do. Her maternal instinct tells her she needs to sacrifice for her children and stay, but on the other hand she has passed through tons of suffering, degradation and unacceptable things for any human being.

Mentally, she feels out of balance and incapable of continuing being functional. Her mental stage is overly altered and nothing consoles her but the idea of having a new life with Paul, but of course, including her children.

When Ana Laura looks at the time, she says good bye to Blanca in a hurry telling her that it was late and she was sure Ramiro had called several times already asking for her. Rushing she gets with Paul in the car and he rushes to take her downtown to get back to the house.

Ana Laura already had called Marcelita and she had anticipated of the extreme anger in which Ramiro was in lately.

She is nervous, nothing links her to him anymore but somehow she feels enslaved to that man.

When she gets home, she hears the phone. She knows it is Ramiro again.

"Hello, yes?"

"I am the one, mother f….. If you think because you're divorced you can do whatever you want, you are wrong. But right now, I am straightening you out." saying this, he hung up the phone.

THE INVISIBLE DOOR
Mireya Mudd

Now Ana Laura starts shaking for she knows he is coming to the house to see her and bring his misery and upset to her life.

She tries to pretend before her children who are in bed that everything is fine. They want to watch television but anticipating the events, she tells them that for today it is better if they go to sleep.

She listens to the claxon at the garage and very fast she listens to some steps approaching, steps that are very familiar to her. They seem like giant steps, going up, approaching fast, going up, each step seems like the house is shaking. The house noises now increases her fear. She tries to relax remembering that the man couldn't hurt her anymore; neither could he have any command over her.

"Where are you cabrona? I just came to remind you of some rules and regulations. If you want to follow them it will be fine but if not you will lose your children."

"But, the children are grown up now," she says, "they were not alone, they were with Marcelita."

THE INVISIBLE DOOR
Mireya Mudd

"Look, you whore, let's make everything clear, you need to be at home at nine o'clock, whether you are married or not. I already have a detective following your steps and seeing that you follow the rules. If not he will be a witness in front of the judge and the child care will pass to me. Is this clear? Eh? Is it clear?"

"But now I am in charge of them, you cannot continue chasing me around. Now I am independent. Anyhow, I always take care of them. I pick them up at school on time. I do their homework with them and I feed them. I talk to them. What else do you want? You cannot command my life anymore."

"That's something we will see. Get out of here, mother f…., and I don't want you to step in this house anymore." While saying this he is pushing her and throwing her down the stairs. The woman is holding herself strongly from the rail and shouts. "Remember, you are putting me out in the street. On another day I will come for my luggage. This is too much, more then a human being can stand. I have tolerated your insults and attacks for several years and I am

THE INVISIBLE DOOR
Mireya Mudd

not doing this anymore. Do you hear me?" Ana Laura feels a big impotence, crying and screaming she doesn't have the ability to make him reasonable.

"Get out of here, you bitch, and I don't want to see you around here anymore….."

THE INVISIBLE DOOR
Mireya Mudd

CHAPTER TWENTY ONE
A nightmare that never ends

Ana Laura tries not to think much. She knows the thoughts of abandoning this terrible situation have been in her mind for many years and now she believes it is the right moment. She knows she cannot be weak. She dresses using her raincoat that is hanging in the coat rack to cover her pajamas. She gets into the car and puts the gear in reverse. She sees Ramiro chasing after her trying to reach her. "Just remember bitch, mother f..., if you go, you go," and saying this he throws a lit cigarette in her lap.

The woman reacts very quickly. She grabs the cigarette and sends it back to him, not giving him much time to react. She is backing up in the car and Ramiro reaches her saying. "This car stays here, cabrona," and grabbing the keys to the car he doesn't allow her to continue her escape. "Get out of the car, now bitch, get out."

Following this, he pushes her out of the garage door, leaving her in the street. Closing the door, yes, the door to her freedom, the consolation door, the door that will

THE INVISIBLE DOOR
Mireya Mudd

disconnect her from her misery, the door that tells her, *yes, get out of here, get out, or he will kill you.*

Crying beside the door in the street in her nightgown covered by her raincoat, ashamed of not having anything to cover her but that old raincoat, she feels the air of the night and that relaxes her. How humiliating and what to do now? How can she get her children and just run to the end of the world? How can she support their careers without money, without a career of her own, without anything?

Ana Laura somehow knows she is subjected to stay close to Ramiro since nothing can take her away from her children. They are her adoration. On the other hand she knows her mental stage is getting worse. She wants to cry for anything and any situation makes her feel very lonesome, unprotected, and practically of no functional use.

She has to drag herself to go everyday and teach since her energy is disturbed by terrible feelings of terror, anxiety and feelings of insecurity for her well being.

After this incident Marcelita opens the main door for her and she spends the night in the living room.

THE INVISIBLE DOOR
Mireya Mudd

THE INVISIBLE DOOR
Mireya Mudd

CHAPTER TWENTY TWO
Discussing options & acceptance

Next day Ana Laura goes to a coffee shop in downtown Taxco. On the typical street of *Truco,* she wants to cry and talk with Paul who is at the moment also downtown. Both want to talk about their future and her children's future.

This place of town has always inspired her some sense of tranquility since you can see art work from different famous artists hanging on the walls and at the same time one could listen to classical music.

However, this time it is different for her stage of anguish is a nightmare, just to think about not being able to take her children with her petrifies her.

Ana Laura and Paul talked for several hours. First, they think about her living far away from Ramiro, maybe in Mexico City where she could ask for a job with her sister who is the owner of a Language Academy. A second possibility, they think about having a small apartment close to Ramiro's home in order to see her children everyday. Since Ramiro had a section in the divorce papers that specified that the children should remain in his home. She remembers Ramiro's words. "My children are not going to live in a shack, so, while you stay here you can still take care of the children. Otherwise they will remain here."

Ana Laura knows how Ramiro manipulated the situation while getting the divorce and how he had formatted the divorce papers in conjunction with a lawyer at his own convenience. She remembers how stupid she acted while signing the divorce papers; how she signed really fast just to get rid of the man without consulting a lawyer before and without reading the document carefully.

Ana Laura does not want to leave her children and feels terribly unhappy. Now, not only is she thinking of leaving her home in America but Paul would live away from her.

Paul and she know well that is not the solution either. Now everything is getting more complicated, Ana Laura knows her son Andrés doesn't want to go with her if she leaves, since he is in a deep stage of anger towards her.

Andrés is very scared of losing her and that's why he is reacting so angry. However, Ana Laura needs to resolve the

THE INVISIBLE DOOR
Mireya Mudd

situation which anguishes her and saddens her tremendously since she knows how difficult it would be to live without them. She also knows she cannot survive with Ramiro's abuses and needs to take care of her mental wellbeing.

On the other hand Rodrigo has told her that if it is necessary, he will depart with her. She remembers his words. "I hate him. Why doesn't he leave this house and leave us alone? I hope he leaves and never comes back."

On several occasions Rodrigo saw his mother being abused. He has been her strength and shelter. Rodrigo has a very severe weight issue because of taking care of his mother every time he has seen her crying. Sometimes, she didn't want to involve him on her hurt but she couldn't pretend and she could understand the severe damage the abuse was creating on both children.

Finally, after a long conversation with Paul, they decided that the best way was to get married and fight to get custody of her children.

THE INVISIBLE DOOR
Mireya Mudd

That evening they arranged a meeting with Ramiro to talk about their decision.

Ana Laura cried for several hours without being able to get any consolation, knowing she would not be happy unless her children left with her.

Paul is comforting her with tenderness and supports her firmly saying. "Everything will be all right, think about this; one of these days we will be together enjoying life with your children and we will be very happy. You'll see, one of these days we will be laughing about this big mess."

* * *

Many years have passed-by since that day. Ana Laura departed with Paul from the little town of Taxco without her children. Living without her children has been a constant torture and which she conformed by writing poems to feel healing and to give some sense of tranquility to her anguish.

When her children talked to Ramiro, being scared of changes, they have accepted to stay with him. This acceptance has broken Ana Laura's heart but her limit to resistance was at the top and for her own mental health she took the decision of leaving with Paul.

Ramiro offered Andrés a brand new car just when he turned fifteen and he accepted the bribe even though he didn't have enough common sense at that age to make the right decision.

Rodrigo, on the other hand was afraid of telling his dad that he wanted to go with his mother. So, he accepted staying with his mean father knowing that it will give some peace of mind that his mother was safe. This was the only purpose for Rodrigo, to see his mom safe without being abused or tortured.

In other words he sacrificed himself to keep the peace between his dad and his mom. Rodrigo knows that this way his dad will leave his mom alone.

One day, a year after this incident, Rodrigo writes a letter to his mom.

I am writing this letter to tell you what a great time we had with you. I have realized how much I love you and how

THE INVISIBLE DOOR
Mireya Mudd

much you are capable of doing for us, so we are happy and well.

I know sometimes I don't express what I feel for you, but always remember and do not doubt that I love you very much, and the same as for you, what makes me most happy is that you are not sad and that you don't suffer for our fault, or because we are faraway. Remember, we are your children and that you and I will never be away from each other, even with the distance that separates us. Even if you don't believe it, I remember perfectly how many special times we spent together, good and bad, but, at the end, those bad situations helped to join us more and that's why we love each other so much and we will always be one for the other.

Now, here in Taxco, I am tranquil and live in peace thinking that you are too.

When you are alone, remember that I think about you and I love you very, very much.

To end this letter, I want to thank you for all what you have done for us and more then anything for me, your

THE INVISIBLE DOOR
Mireya Mudd

advising, your love for us and your union with me for being the best mother in this world.

With love,

Rodrigo

Many years passed by and Ana Laura's suffering continued to be unbearable, since she missed her children so much and she writes:

(It rhymes in Spanish)

June 1998

Burning feelings that

Agitate my being

I would like to avoid it

So that I don't suffer anymore

It's being two years

Of big suffering

Leaving my loves

My heart has broken

For my well being I departed

Like a fish that runs away;

I needed to get away

THE INVISIBLE DOOR
Mireya Mudd

in order to grow

Stepped on like a dog

I used to be in that cage

Everyone's servant

Sacrificing everyday

One day that door

smiled at me suspiciously

and a new light shake my whole being.

Uncertainty came to me,

am I doing the right thing?

So I told to myself;

Love yourself and others will

love you,

and looking at the light

I decided to leave...

Now, after many years

I can see with determination

My self-esteem has grown

My children look at me with admiration

THE INVISIBLE DOOR
Mireya Mudd

And a profound pride

illuminates my path......

I have given them strength

to grow stronger

I have inspirited their daily life

Teaching them how hard is to survive

And both have acquired their independence

knowing now clearly

How to survive...

Now they are warriors

Ready to fight

The incandescent fight

Of the difficult live...

My children

I love you with deep value

And remember my children

That now,

You are oaks.....

THE INVISIBLE DOOR
Mireya Mudd

THE INVISIBLE DOOR
Mireya Mudd

CHAPTER TWENTY THREE
A healing of time

The years truly cure most everything and Paul was right that Ana Laura could not foresee other new problems coming into her life. Yes, life always has a lot of unexpected complexities that makes people take precipitous decisions; some made without analyzing the consequences. New contradictions would come to Paul and Ana Laura as a couple, however, the problems would never be similar to the impulsive violence and anger from her first husband.

Ana Laura suffered for two years continuously until she realized that her children were alright and had overcome her departure.

She remembers that first summer in which Paul and she arrived to Athens, West Virginia, after departing from Taxco. They were going to spend a summer in a *summer camp* were Paul was going to teach English and Literature.

That was so difficult for Ana Laura. Paul used to go early to teach and she stayed in a very small three by four room crying, reading and missing her children. Ana Laura loved Paul profoundly and that consoled her. Paul used to constantly go to see her and help her cope with her feelings of losing her children and talked to her and comforted her. They talked for hours.

She remembers Paul telling her. "Look Ana Laura, I know very well what you are passing through. It is not easy. The decision you took is very difficult, but you did this for your own mental wellbeing and your children's. They prefer to see you safe than seeing you in a dangerous situation and your life at risk."

"I know," she says, "but I miss them and one day they will hate me for not forcing them to come live with me."

"Not at all," Paul says, "Look Ana Laura, they are better off like this, than seeing you suffering. You know that more than anybody. One day they will admire you for being strong and for not tolerating to be stepped on and manipulated by that mean man. Also, one day they will follow you, you will see. Weak people are never admired, but for somebody who knows how to protect her rights, she will have their respect and love. You know that, you will see."

Paul was right and the years proved that to her. After years beyond these events, her children loved her and admired her as nobody could. On many occasions, she has talked to them and they supported her and venerated her and their love for her has grown.

One day, she remembers Rodrigo's words who told her." Look mom, the day that you left, you took away a heavy weight from me. I knew I was going to miss you a lot, and it was going to be very difficult not seeing you, but, on the other hand it was a relief to see you safe and that's the only thing I worried about. So, don't complain for having left us. Look, now you have a career and a master's degree and that's admirable. Now you don't have to depend on anyone to survive. You don't know how much I admire you and love you."

While hearing this, Ana Laura couldn't do anything but cry out of happiness and for the first time she felt relieved. Her children admired and recognized her.

THE INVISIBLE DOOR
Mireya Mudd

One afternoon, Ana Laura writes a poem for her children, inspiring them to be strong and to progress in life:

(It rhymes in Spanish)

THE CHILDREN

You nurtured the seed

You let them fly

You didn't block them

You let them be...

If you look for them

Because you need them

Like a star without rout

You will miss the path.

Reflecting internal peace

Like a refreshing landscape,

Transmitting tenderness

Projecting peace;

They will look for you.......

THE INVISIBLE DOOR
Mireya Mudd

THE INVISIBLE DOOR
Mireya Mudd

CHAPTER TWENTY FOUR
Beginning of another ending

The incidents in her second marriage were coming more frequently. Ana Laura sensed that Paul was not satisfied with his marriage, after all, he had been single for sixteen years after his first marriage and the adaptation to a new marriage was very complicated. Their fights could not be compared at all with the ones from her first marriage.

So, one day Ana Laura writes in her dairy:

"Again we went to Frostburg at *Gandalph Restaurant* to have dinner with Paul's daughter Hannah. Typical Mediterranean food, pleasant environment, dishes decorated artistically, but a humble restaurant. We enjoyed each others company and talked about our problems. Also mentioned Paul's new play in which he is working on at the moment about, *The Heaven and Hell*.

And what happened there to Ana Laura was still remembered vividly.

"Paul and Ana Laura went to a bar close to the restaurant to continue talking with Hannah. After some

THE INVISIBLE DOOR
Mireya Mudd

time Hannah said goodbye and left. Paul and she decided to take a walk on the streets and while approaching their car, they started to argue because she said while she was pointing to another Restaurant: "One day I would like to come and eat at that French Restaurant." and Paul answered rudely. "I hope you have money to pay for the meal!" At that moment she started to recall other incidents similar to that in which Paul was refusing to pay.

Ana Laura knows very well it is the American life in which couples pay fifty, fifty and they share all the expenses.

She did not grow-up in that kind of sharing system and she feels disconcerted without knowing how to proceed or what to do.

On another occasion she mentioned of wanting to go to Europe. He answered that there was no reason to go unless for an artistic project or similar motive. She told him, she'd go by herself and didn't need anything from him.

After that incident in Frostburg they got into the car and Paul starts saying. "You are selfish." Ana Laura doesn't know where all this is coming from and she replied. "If you think so, there is no reason to stay together," They argued for a long time and slept together like two strangers, turning each others backs while sleeping and saying it was about time to start the divorce process.

That morning they talked again about divorce but while talking they made up.

Ana Laura is talking alone. "Human beings are very complex. I have many mixed feelings and this scares me to death. Sometimes I love Paul dearly with deep love and admiration, but other times I want to run away from him and get another job and disappear. This will cause a situation of temporary pain and will transform into a deep suffering full of acute pain that will last for a long time."

She continues. "Paul's deep sense of realism makes me suffer since I am a profound romantic. It hurts me that he judges me so objectively. That gives me deep pain."

She knows that in every relationship there is pain involved, but in her first marriage it was physically present at all times. It was obvious Ramiro was the one producing

THE INVISIBLE DOOR
Mireya Mudd

that pain, but now, in her second marriage she knows pain is always there even if there is no domestic violence involved.

Ana Laura is feeling very lonesome and without a sense of orientation to new goals and all that Paul had provided at the beginning was not there anymore. Everything was different now. There was not the same connection anymore and the conversations between them were getting smaller everyday. Paul began to isolate himself from her to get his space.

One evening Paul went to one of his poetry reading sessions. He refused to take Ana Laura and so, she writes in her dairy:

November 14, 2000:

My life continues wandering with no route. Everything is uncertain and I am not sure about which consequences this can bring.

I feel like a wind compass without direction.

I see you and don't know you anymore, since you still are new.

THE INVISIBLE DOOR
Mireya Mudd

Your being has shut down like a coffin and it is impossible to read you anymore.

I still will come to you since I need you intensively.

And something tells me, you are not the one I need, so, I continue searching, without a fixed route my soul is empty, in a vacuum, without illusions.

She continues writing, this time a poem in Spanish:

Empty path, without rout,

a desolated route that demands me to grow.

The world steps on you and it scatters like sand,

But you don't fall apart; you don't let that affect you.

Your strength is immense and you continue implacable, solid,

you don't allow anything to defeat you.

Your strength is needed for the human survival

and you know that nothing or anybody will defeat you…

* * *

THE INVISIBLE DOOR
Mireya Mudd

Many years passed by in which Ana Laura feels Paul is getting more distant from her. One night she talks to him and asks him on the phone "Who are you? I don't know you anymore."

This produces Paul's anger and he answers in an angry way saying he was not going to tolerate the way she always questioned him. He continued saying he didn't feel free and this was causing him to stop communicating with her.

She was very angry and asked why every Tuesday when he stayed in Petersburg, that he needed to go to the bar?

Paul answered very aggressive saying. "I don't have to give you any explanations. I hate control."

Ana Laura understood immediately that Paul was a free spirit man and nobody and nothing could tie him to a situation in which he felt a prisoner.

That night they had a big fight in which she asked him why was he still with her if he was so unhappy. She continued saying that from now on she wouldn't ask anything about his life, since he gets infuriated about her questions.

After that Paul wanted to change the subject. He asked her how her day was and she answered. "From today forward, I won't inform you about my life, or of what I did during the day!"

Communication was lost...

That evening when Ana Laura came back from work, seeing Paul taking his nap. She says. "This morning while I was reading my last summer diary, I observed how we have had several conflicts in our marriage."

Paul answered very angry. "I am considering a separation, since nobody is going to take my freedom away from me."

A sharp pain comes to Ana Laura's chest. In her heart she is feeling a sense of abandonment and impotence at the same time. She feels like death is tearing her apart after a long agony. Slowly she disengages her feelings from being beside Paul and she feels her tears dry. She cannot cry

THE INVISIBLE DOOR
Mireya Mudd
    anymore and she feels ready for the breakup.

THE INVISIBLE DOOR
Mireya Mudd

CHAPTER TWENTY FIVE
Middle pages to the ending

Several months passed by and Paul and Ana Laura go to visit Paul's sister in Michigan. Without mentioning the divorce subject, she writes again in her dairy:

November, 1999:

Yesterday I was so happy and I expressed this to Paul. I told him I was so happy because I loved him.

Right after saying this he started an argument. "Your love is false because your love implies a manipulation. You only love if you can manipulate your loved one, and that's why it is not real."

I told him. "I agree, but don't tell me your love is unconditional because I doubt that answer."

I was very sad to see he didn't consider me a true love but, in some way, I understood. I believe the only unconditional love is a mother's love, one that comes without any expectations.

Later on he tried to make it up to me, but it was difficult for the day was already soured.

THE INVISIBLE DOOR
Mireya Mudd

We went to a basketball game in which his brother-in-law is the trainer and I was very indifferent with Paul. It is unbelievable how human nature is when humans protect from being hurt. When there is an inevitable situation in order to survive a love pain; it is like when the person you love is dying, there is no remedy and nothing to be done...

So, Ana Laura continues writing:

Now we are in Cadillac, we are staying at Paul's brother's home and his sister-in-law. My days have been difficult because I don't trust Paul anymore and I feel him to be distant.

Yesterday we walked beside the lake and we agreed on him spending the night with his friend Jim (from Michigan).

After that he told me. "On second thought, I better stay and sleep at Jim's home, so you don't have to come and get me so late."

I thought. If I make a big scene here, it is going to be worse, so I said. "It's all right, tomorrow I'll pick you up at nine in the morning and we can go out for breakfast."

THE INVISIBLE DOOR
Mireya Mudd

It is five in the morning, I am in this strange home of Paul's brother and I haven't been able to sleep thinking about Paul. He gave me one hundred dollars so I could go shopping for Christmas, and so I would not complain about his outings with his friend Jim. I feel he has guilt feelings and therefore he felt splendid giving me the money, however my jealousy is unsupported.

His brother and sister's in law's home is a strange environment for me since I have never stayed here before and I feel terrible lonesome.

I sometimes think if Paul wants to sleep in another place that he doesn't want to do anything with me, but I can't think like that. Occasionally I would like to have a traditional husband.

Yesterday I went alone to the movie theater and I saw so many couples together and I thought that it was sad that Paul and I need to do our activities separate from each other. Paul frequently goes to a group of lectures and he insists in not taking me with him. He says I don't read books and I don't have any purpose to be there. However,

THE INVISIBLE DOOR
Mireya Mudd

with my college studies I cannot do so much or read more than what I have to do already, so I have to avoid going with him.

Maybe I don't have the courage to leave him?

I have to sleep. Maybe my dreams will help me solve the impossible....

THE INVISIBLE DOOR
Mireya Mudd

CHAPTER TWENTY SIX
An ending is near

Ana Laura and Paul arrive back to West Virginia. They now live in Keyser. She has a new job where she is the dorm director for young girls in college.

Paul starts being more indifferent with Ana Laura. When he comes back from work he almost doesn't talk anymore. He sits quietly and plays solitary for hours and hours and has little to say to her.

One day she decides to confront him about her feelings of rejection and lack of communication that are driving her crazy. She still loves Paul, but she knows this cannot be sustained forever. Each word, each movement that they exchange hurts her like a stabbing wound.

The distance is inevitable, no doubt about it. Ana Laura complains desperately and she asks Paul. "Can you tell me what is going on?" and Paul responds. "We have never communicated, you don't listen to me."

THE INVISIBLE DOOR
Mireya Mudd

"But, tell me, what is going on? You don't love me anymore? I can change; tell me what do you want me to listen to and do?"

With Paul's apathy and his silence, she gets refuge in her books and in her writing. At the same time her solitude grows each day and her fantasies begin. She feels a sense of abandonment which hurt her like a stabbing. Sometimes she wants to shake Paul so that he could reflect and love her again, but when love is indifferent, it is impossible to recover.

She was yearning to find somebody who could tell her how important she was for him, how much he loved her and how much she depended on him to be happy.

* * *

A major change was agreed upon. She and Paul decided to see each other only Thursdays, Fridays and Saturdays. Paul was living in Petersburg where he taught literature at the college and he came to her with his dirty clothes for washing. The new plan was fascinating because it reunited them. They went out dancing and philosophizing. A new

THE INVISIBLE DOOR
Mireya Mudd

experience was born. Communication had started again.

However, this didn't last a long time, since Paul started to show her how important was his freedom. Ana Laura started to feel the distance between them again. She knew Paul's complexity was bigger than hers and she felt all her illusions broken when Paul told her. "I am going for vacation to Taxco. You may go to Taxco with me but I warn you, I am staying one more month."

"What?" The woman answered.

"Yes," Paul precipitates to say, "you cannot stay all the time since you have to come back to work, so, you better buy your ticket to come back one month before me. Otherwise it will cost you more, and I am looking forward to staying there one more month."

Ana Laura knows that Paul's reason to stay there longer is because he has an intimate friend who is a famous artist in Taxco. He is very old and famous and lives with his lover and companion. His lover Silvia flirts aggressively with Paul. When he used to visit them, she was cooking for him and used to isolate herself with Paul to seduce him; but

THE INVISIBLE DOOR
Mireya Mudd

obviously with Ana Laura around, that was not completely possible.

On the other hand, Ana Laura knows that trying to impose and control him is impossible, so she decide to conform to Paul's explanations, which is very good in winning the arguments. So, she decides to come back from her vacation just the way Paul has planned it. She leaves Paul one month in Taxco and she comes back to work in Keyser in her dorm.

** * *

When she comes back to America she decides to write one day:

Poem La Nada (The nothingness)

Opting for life

I dragged my living

I have wished to find

The elixir of life.

Which is the essential fundament of life?

I look for it day and night

Looking for an answer

THE INVISIBLE DOOR
Mireya Mudd

Something tells me then

We are nothing.

Her feelings were of a deep and profound pain and she couldn't reestablish seeing that everything between Paul and her was ending and so one day Ana Laura has feelings of death and desperation and writes:

LA MUERTE (The death)

Like foam we passed

Our consciousness dictates us

Are you important?

Are you significant?

What will be of them without you?

But we are soft warm wind that dissipates

Transforming in a last halo

Gasping full of pain;

Cold wind that dissipates

With the last breath,

Like the thoughts of the one

THE INVISIBLE DOOR
Mireya Mudd

Who sees you depart.......

THE INVISIBLE DOOR
Mireya Mudd

CHAPTER TWENTY SEVEN
Ending

Finally after struggling for a long time, Paul and Ana Laura get a divorce and with her grief she was feeling non-functional, depressed with no zip for life.

The dorm walls reminded her of Paul day by day and so Ana Laura decides to leave that place.

She finds a Spanish teaching job in Maryland. She moves there and works for a year as a teacher for the Quakers who like to meditate and live the simplistic philosophy of life, where nobody should possess more than what they need.

That year was very difficult for her. She used to leave the keys inside of her apartment and needed to call the maintenance people to help her open again. Her mind wandered constantly and she wasn't feeling good.

She cried after working everyday and nothing anybody could do or say could console her.

At the same time she had the need of meeting new people to re-establish her life; so, she used to go to coffee

THE INVISIBLE DOOR
Mireya Mudd

shops and public places to feel that vacuum. However

nothing could console her.

THE INVISIBLE DOOR
Mireya Mudd

CHAPTER TWENTY EIGHT
Be careful of new beginnings

It was the darkest of nights in which she was feeling very sad, heartless, without any inspiration and no will to do anything. For an instance she thought about going back to her apartment, to cry for a while and release her pain and tears, but, on the other hand she decided to stop and eat a pizza and see people.

Ana Laura remembers stopping at the *Stained Glass Pub* and something unexpected happened.

That day she spent the evening with her friend Jimmy in a Vietnamese restaurant. She felt Jimmy was a little depressed since Ana Laura had rejected him. She just wanted him as a friend.

While walking into the Stained Glass Pub, she was observing how many lonely people there are in the world and she hears a woman's voice saying. "Yes, there she is," and pointing at Sophia he continued. "I was waiting for you, you were in my dreams. Do you want to join us? Are you by yourself? Look, this is Marissa."

"Yes," Ana Laura says, "nice to meet you Marissa."

"Well, welcome to the friendly bar. We always like friends."

"Thank you," Ana Laura says.

Marissa continues. "What brings you here"?

"Well, I was heading home and I thought it was still early to enclose myself."

"Same here, Marissa says, welcome to the single, lonely crowd."

As Ana Laura is talking to Marissa she can see how much a gentleman named Dave is staring at her. Dave offers her a gin and tonic and tells the bartender. "She is on me. I will pay for whatever she drinks."

The three of them, Marissa, Dave and Ana Laura spent the evening dancing and laughing. Ana Laura is curious about who they are and suggest for them to sit at a table and talk for a while. They find a table where the music is not so loud.

She asks a couple of questions and finds out Dave is a doctor in the U.S. military. He is very intelligent and can speak for many hours introducing many different subjects. Ana Laura can tell he has a high IQ and it is so nice to be able to talk with somebody who converses about so many topics.

Meanwhile Marissa leaves with a friend that she finds and goes dancing.

They spend a wonderful evening laughing and dancing and after the second drink Ana Laura decides to go back home. Dave, seeing her intentions of leaving approaches her with a napkin and says. "Please write your name and address. I want to see you again if you don't mind."

"Not at all," she says, while she writes just her phone number in the napkin.

"Write your address too," Dave insists.

"No," Ana Laura says, "I don't give my address to anybody."

"OK, but are you sure this is your telephone number?"

"Yes, she says, why would I lie?"

Dave excuses himself to go to the restroom.

THE INVISIBLE DOOR
Mireya Mudd

Marissa suddenly approaches again to Ana Laura and takes the napkin away from her and puts it in her pocket. Marissa approaches her and secretly says to her. "You don't want to date this guy."

"Why not?"

"No, you don't want to date him, just trust me on this one. I will call you later to explain."

Ana Laura thinks to herself. She must be a very jealous and a possessive person. Maybe they have a relationship.

As she is heading out of the Pub, Dave approaches her and says. "Don't leave, I cannot find your telephone number. Please write it here again."

Now Ana Laura is tired and ready to go home, so she rushes to write it down.

It is two in the morning and Ana Laura is coming into her apartment at the Quaker School when she hears the phone ringing.

"Hello?"

"Hi, it's me," a mans voice says.

THE INVISIBLE DOOR
Mireya Mudd

"Who are you"? Ana Laura asks.

"It's me Dave. I was wondering if you would like to go out tomorrow for a dinner and a movie."

"That sounds great,"

"Let's do it."

"I'll call you tomorrow." "How about at 1:30 to make arrangements?"

"Ok, I'll see you tomorrow."

It's 1 P.M, next day when she hears the phone ringing:

"Hi."

"Hi, is this Dave?"

"No, it's John."

"John who?"

"John, the guy you met last night, at the Pub."

"You said you were Dave."

"Well, sometimes I am John too, or Dave, to other people. You know? I have to protect myself from strangers who are after me, so I never tell my real name."

"Oh, I see, but I really need to know who you are."

THE INVISIBLE DOOR
Mireya Mudd

"Let's say I am John for today, you know? I like to make jokes all the time, but I am also paranoiac-schizophrenic and I don't trust anyone."

"Stop kidding, you better tell me the truth. You're scaring me."

"No, it's the truth. The doctors detected this in me a long time ago, but now I am cured. I have been cured for two years now."

"Can this be cured with medication?"

"Of course, can't you see the proof with me?"

"Well…yeah."

"So, at what time can we meet?" He insists.

"Well, I'm going to have dinner with a friend at 7 P.M. I won't be able to go today, but how about meeting for lunch today here in Medford?"

"I'm not ready yet, he says, I just came back from a walk. I need to shower."

"Well, get ready and we can meet at 2 P.M."

"I don't think I can do it that fast, besides I already had lunch."

"Well, I can go ahead and have lunch and wait for you at the coffee shop at the plaza, the Starbuck coffee shop. Is that OK?"

"OK, see you there."

Ana Laura is waiting at the coffee shop. It's been one and a half hours already since she talked to Dave. She is still waiting.

Maybe he couldn't find the place after all. She continues writing in her dairy and she was ready to go when she sees him coming.

"What are you writing?" He asks while approaching.

"Just my dairy."

"So, you like to write eh?"

"Yes, very much, I write everything about my life."

"Come with me," Dave says, "I need an ATM machine to get some money."

"It's all right. I can pay for the coffee."

"No, I still need money since I'm going to the mall later to buy some clothes."

THE INVISIBLE DOOR
Mireya Mudd

They walked towards the bank machines which it is one block away.

Ana Laura stays in the sun waiting for him since she is freezing. It's the beginning of the fall and she needs the sun desperately.

She is very concerned about their conversation on the phone and she has a deep distrust.

As she sees him coming back, she decides to confront him asking directly what is going on with him. Is he really paranoiac-schizophrenic? Is he really cured? She needs to protect herself in her vulnerable situation of being single.

"Dave."

"Am I Dave?" he asks

"You told me that was your name!"

"Well, I don't know if I told you Dave or John, you see? You cannot trust anyone…"

"Yeah……. I know," pretending she agrees. "Tell me who you are," she insists with a desperate tone.

"I just like to joke that my name is Dave."

THE INVISIBLE DOOR
Mireya Mudd

"I am never going to know who you are if you are joking all the time?"

"Are you really a paranoiac-schizophrenic?"

His face turned red. Ana Laura knows now she is making him angry, but she still insists, since he is changing the subject all time.

"Please, she says, tell me if it's true."

"Of course, I am, but I told you, I'm cured…Let's go to the mall, come with me."

"No, we were going to meet for coffee, not for shopping."

"Well, my original plan was to go to the mall, but since you changed it and I was planning to buy something why don't you come with me? Come on, let's go in my car."

"No, thanks," she says as she sees him standing up determined to go. "You go, I also have many chores to do at home. You better go by yourself."

"No, no, please wait, you just don't know who I am."

"Come on, I will never know who you are."

"Well, do you really want to know who I am?"

THE INVISIBLE DOOR
Mireya Mudd

"Of course."

"I am God, and I have special powers. I am the second Christ that the Catholics are waiting for. Have you heard about it?"

"Yes.......so, who is your mother. Is she the Virgin Mary?"

"Yes, except she is not virgin, she's a slut. She can fuck six men at one time."

Ana Laura doesn't know what to do. She knows she cannot express fear because that's what he wants, so, she tries to remain calm.

She asks. "Tell me why did you divorce your wife? What drew you apart?"

"I got tired of her nagging at me all the time."

"So, that's why you divorced her?"

"I didn't divorce her, I killed her."

* * *

Now Ana Laura wants desperately out of this situation, but she has read a lot of psychology books and worked at a

THE INVISIBLE DOOR
Mireya Mudd

Crisis Response Unit and knows what to do. She tries to stay calm.

"So, tell me, how did you kill her?"

"I injected something in her."

"Come on, don't tell me that. You know, I want to be your friend, so, please tells me the truth."

"I don't like friends."

"Why?"

"I get tired of them and then I want to kill them too."

Now, she is extremely nervous, she excuses herself saying." I'm going to the restroom."

While she gets up she puts all her belongings in her purse.

"Don't you try to sneak away like many people that I know have done?"

"Don't worry," she says, "of course I'm not leaving. I'm just going to the bathroom."

THE INVISIBLE DOOR
Mireya Mudd

"Before you go let me tell you, I can prove to you right now that I am God. I can be on the other side of this window in a minute." He continues, "Don't be scared, I wouldn't kill you since you are a sinner."

"What makes me a sinner?"

"That you don't go to church, plus you are not involved in a spiritual life, so, you are not ready to die. Otherwise, you will go to hell."

"I see, and I'm happy. I'm not ready to die. Anyway, I'm very spiritual since I perceived human needs but I will tell you about that later. I need to go…see you in a bit."

"Wait, do you know my friend, Will? He is also here?"

"Where?"

"He's right here, but nobody can see him."

"Oh, tell me where is he?"

"Right here," he says, as he points to the lower part of his leg. "He's wrapped to me down here with a rubber band. He's my best friend and he protects me from my enemies."

THE INVISIBLE DOOR
Mireya Mudd

"OK, Ana Laura says, we'll talk about Will when I come back."

Ana Laura goes to the restroom, she is uncertain about leaving since she doesn't want to infuriate him. Anyway, there is no exit in the back of the coffee shop. She thinks about calling 911 and many possibilities but cannot think right. She is scared, terrified and her brain is not helping.

She comes back to the table, but she cannot sit back down. She says impulsively, "I have to go, I really need to go. I have a bunch of stuff to do at home."

As they are walking out of Starbucks, she thanks him for the coffee and she can see his face is very red. He is angry.

She walks quickly towards her car, while seeing him following her. She jumps in her car and locks herself in and starts crying.

THE INVISIBLE DOOR
Mireya Mudd

SUMMARY

July 27, 2001

Ana Laura listens to the quietness of her home and observes what used to terrify her is now a delightful experience. How she loves silence.

She remembers a few months ago she was scared in the house with the presence of silence.

Now she enjoys the solitude. It is sacred and it gives her a sense of protection.

She knows in the past she pressured Paul to stay with her since it was difficult to stay alone. However, now she didn't need him or anybody.

At the same time being involved in another culture has been very difficult plus being away from her children, their laughs, their voices, their games, they were the ones who had inundated Ana Laura's life with happiness for sixteen years. But now, she is trying to avoid the past or the future and has learned through suffering how to enjoy the moment. There is no doubt that life is a constant learning experience, she thinks.

THE INVISIBLE DOOR
Mireya Mudd

It is a hard life and she has to adapt to live alone and to be alone without depending on anyone. She tells herself that it is better to be alone than with the wrong person and so, she keeps looking for a companion. She needs to grow up and become more independent and self-sufficient. It is the only way of becoming successful.

When she was younger she remembered how men could do what they wanted, without being questioned. On the contrary, women needed to do everything according to family rules where men were protected somehow. But on the other side they needed to support the women and keep the family together and ahead of everything which she did not think was expected in an American family.

All this psychology contributed to expect more from men. She could not understand this concept until one day when she started to feel self-sufficient and only depended on herself. She had so high expectations on men and from now on she would need to do it alone, but with a lot of pride, finally she would be able to feel equal.

THE INVISIBLE DOOR
Mireya Mudd

There were many loves in her life and she suffered and enjoyed a lot from these experiences, but something was clear in her mind as she said to herself. *I depend only on myself and nobody else. I was born alone and will die alone.* Only these thoughts helped the woman inside Ana Laura recover confidence and gave her security. Now she doesn't believe in true love but she thinks it is only a manipulation from both sides to control the other person and that is what people call *love*.

Only accepting the other person the way they are could be a real and unique relationship. Ana Laura had tried to change her loved ones, or she had the false illusion that love could transform people, but now, she can see everything clearly. When she meets somebody new she needs to like his personality, his thoughts, and his feelings and accept the person the way he is, otherwise it will never work out.

Since then she analyzes everyone carefully and she knows what they like and what they don't like, and if there are any differences she stays away from them, since the

THE INVISIBLE DOOR
Mireya Mudd

inevitable end will come.

After all, the saying goes *"Mas sabe el diablo por viejo, que por diablo."* Which means…The devil knows more for being old than for being the Devil.

She knew this was a new beginning, a beginning that gave her a lot of hope and happiness. Now the **door is not invisible** anymore. She always thought she was never going to be able to coexist alone, but how wrong was she. Now she knew the reality and more then anything she believed in herself.

Many doors down her road of life were going to open for her.

Made in the USA
Charleston, SC
07 July 2012